NOT IN MY NAME

Why representative democracy has to end now.

Compiled by Simon Mitchell

Compiled and produced at simonthescribe

simonthescribe.co.uk

Contents

Preface

'*Not In My Name*' is about changing from the representative democracies that we have in the UK and US to participatory democracies. This book gives a case for why it needs to happen urgently. It describes how it might happen and what you can do to help bring it about – if you consider such a thing desirable – and this book aims to persuade you of such.

'*Not In My Name*' is a plea for you to think, to really think whether we need this endless stream of self-interested politicians (mostly) called 'government', of whatever party, dominating every single aspect of our choices, mis-representing what we think, do, eat, and dream? It is a cry for our personal liberation to evolve as humans and a recognition of our capacity for taking personal responsibility for our own lives.

Capitalism has failed along with its 'representative democracy'. Successive government's single-mindedness to support it has taken our environment – our ability to sustain the conditions for life on earth – to the edge of a precipice. The influence of human activity on Planet Earth has started the Sixth Mass Extinction. Like any sensible person I would prefer this journey of our culture to 'a new way of relating to the earth', to be a gradual transition in which as few people suffer as possible.

I am not going to make any apologies here about the large number of quotations and extractions in this book. This is a book 'written with a hundred pens'. It is not an academic paper. I am not going to re-word what people much cleverer than me have already written in order to claim it as my own.

My role as compiler of '*Not In My Name*' is to integrate the pre-existing ideas contained within into a cohesive and structured argument to help you, the reader, see what is going on, what is being hidden in front of your face and to help you decide what level of involvement to take in creating a future for us all.

1. THE PURPOSE OF HUMANS

"It is surely our responsibility to do everything within our power to create a planet that provides a home, not just for us, but for all life on earth".

Sir David Attenborough, Blue Planet

'Adapt or die' was an early rule of human evolution and humans did well. More opportunistic than foxes, cleverer than monkeys, their adaptable fingers soon found tools to wield, smashing apart the bones of dead creatures to drink the life-giving marrow that other animals couldn't reach. In the Anthropocene Era humans were a triumph. In the blink of the Universe's eye, they had changed the rules, finding security in tribes, they adapted their harsh environment to suit themselves by building dwellings, then over time towering edifices spreading across the land. They ordered and controlled the beasts to maximise their own food production, laying waste to the woods and forests in vast swathes of lifeless monoculture made for their own convenience.

Humans were a triumph of evolution but now we have changed our own circumstances and are failing to adapt to the effects of these self-inflicted changes.

But what is it that makes us tick? Is there a point to us humans? One thing that isn't really asked very much at school, in work, at play, at home is the question 'What are human beings actually for?' Once you start asking this question you may be drawn towards (and often hijacked) by existing religion, philosophy, mysticism, strange cults or whatever takes your fancy. But this is an important question and one that doesn't get enough airplay.

If you look at some of the amazing things humans have done you can't fail to be blown away by just how brilliant we can be. Stupendous inventions, utterly beautiful art, completely transcendental music, unbelievable technology that does fantastic things. Acts of love and bravery beyond comprehension. At our best we are utterly beautiful beings capable of deep compassion, humility, sheer genius, absolute brilliance.

But we also have our dark side, a side that leads us to lay waste to our own planet in order to create financial riches for a few insecure people. A side that destroys without thought, sometimes without even noticing, in order to further our own objectives. The cruelty and ignorance of humans can be despicable. What is our story with that?

Martin Winiecki, coordinator of the Terra Nova School in Tamera Center, Portugal describes the normal 'story of consumerism' we are conditioned to act out;

"What is the dream of the Western world? When asked, most young people say: A perfect partner, a beautiful house, successful career, lots of money and travel to exotic places. Amplified a million times a day by Hollywood and the advertisement industry, promoted by parents, self-help gurus, schools and fairytales, this lifestyle became the central motif of our collective longing, the blueprint of globalized society.

Fulfillment became a matter of possession, of how much wealth, fame, power and sex we earned for ourselves. Rewarding people with profit and status for the most competitive and destructive behavior, worshiping the golden calf of maximal economic growth, capitalism has effectively manufactured and then exploited people's dream image. Humanity's general ethical decline is the result of this collective corruption."

The motivating 'Dream of the Western World' as described above is a trap based on a fundamental flaw – a house built on sand. An illusion created to move us into human slavery. It ties us to a base and minimal expression of our capabilities as human beings.

One problem is that when our stories of capitalism were made, population was relatively small and nature seemed abundant. This led us to believe that nature was an infinite resource we could plunder forever. All of its 'inputs' such as cross pollination by bees, fields of grass grown with soil and sunshine, the action of yeast on sugar, the coal and oil and diamonds waiting underground, were, and are still often deemed as 'free'.

'We can, if need be, ransack the whole globe, penetrate into the bowels of the earth, descend to the bottom of the deep, travel to the farthest regions of this world, to acquire wealth.'

William Derham, 'Physio-Theology', 1713

All this free stuff was so ready for the taking that they did not even have an associated value on the balance sheets (apart from the cost of extraction). Hence capitalism was born as a lie because it has been using what are fundamentally capital assets, the natural resources of the planet, as income, ever since it came into being. And now the population is huge and its exploitable assets are drying up.

The cost of exploiting dirty energy like oil, coal or fracking for example now has such a large associated cost of damage to the ecosystem, that it is more beneficial overall to leave it in the ground. However much proof about solar or wind energy being 'cheaper' is provided, the huge corporations do not want to hear that fossil fuel sources might become 'stranded assets'.

"Many people who are going through the early stages of the awakening process are no longer certain what their outer purpose is. What drives the world no longer drives them. Seeing the madness of our civilisation so clearly, they feel somewhat alienated from the culture around them. Some feel that they inhabit a no-man's-land between two worlds. They are no longer run by the ego, yet the arising awareness has not yet become fully integrated into their lives. Inner and outer purposes have not merged."

Eckhart Tolle

In 'Free to be Human' David Edwards, claims we are held in 'powerful psychological chains' by this 'Dream of the Western World' which severely limits our capability to see properly:

"This is a book about freedom, and above all about the idea that there is often no greater obstacle to freedom than the assumption that it has already been fully attained. While in the West few individuals today suffer physical restraint by the state, we are still constrained by powerful psychological chains - which in many ways are far more effective, if only because they are so difficult to perceive.

Free to be Human shows how the same filter system (corporately controlled mass media hegemony) distorts our understanding of many personal, ethical and spiritual issues, ensuring that we remain passive, conformist, confused and uninformed - and willing to accept the irrational values of corporate consumerism.

David Edwards argues that, in order to counter this continual process of disinformation and disempowerment, we need to master the arts of 'intellectual self defence' and so become able to challenge the deceptions of a system that subordinates people and planet to the drive for profit".

Edwards D. Free to be Human. Intellectual Self-defense in an Age of Illusions. Resurgence Books. 1995 (blurb)

Motivation to Breathe

Abraham Maslow's 'Model of Human Needs', shows a motivating hierarchy that might explain why we behave the way we do. It has been a strong influence in understanding our culture since the 1950's. It is used in advertising to predict and manipulate people's needs and motivations, in health and social services as a sort of scale of personal well-being and in cultural and business studies as a reference to personal development in relation to employment.

Maslow's original model shows a hierarchy of human needs that start at the bottom and work upwards.

1. Basic physiological needs – to be able to eat, drink and maintain physical integrity, air, food, drink, shelter, warmth, sex, sleep, etc. Once we have attained these basic needs we can progress to;

2. Safety needs – freedom from attack, from extreme environmental conditions, security, order, law, limits, stability, etc. Then to;

3. Social needs – to have a sense of belonging to a group, tribe, work group, family, affection, relationships, etc. These lead on to;

4. Esteem needs – the need to derive some positive value from our actions, self-esteem, achievement, mastery, independence, status, dominance, prestige, managerial responsibility, etc. Then:

5. Self-actualisation needs – the need to 'become who you are' – self-fulfilment, realising personal potential, seeking personal growth and peak experiences.

Maslow states that until one level of need is fulfilled that the person is unlikely to move on to the next, for example if you are hungry and thirsty and have nowhere to live you are unlikely to be looking for social status. He suggests that each need has to be aroused and unsatisfied to be a motivating force in behaviour.

Watching adverts on TV it is easy to see how they work to arouse unsatisfied needs at these five levels to motivate people to buy stuff. You 'must have this' in order to 'look cool' to your group (social). 'Protect your family' with this amazing product (safety). You will 'never be happy until' you have this product (esteem).

In fact, happiness isn't very good for the economy. If we were happy with what we had, why would we need more? How do you sell an ant-aging moisturiser? You make someone worry about aging. How to you get someone to vote for a political party? You make them worry about immigration. How do you get them to buy insurance? By making them worry about everything. How do you get them to watch a TV show? By making them worry about missing out. How do you get them to buy a new smartphone? By making them feel they are being left behind.

More common in this age of 'celebrity consumer capitalism' is an appeal to the ego to manipulate 'the perfect you in the process of becoming' (self-actualisation) in the interests of consumerism. Consider, for example, some of these prime values from brand-name adverts:

- Weightwatchers club: **"Be Who You Want To Be"**
- Microsoft: **"Where do you want to go today"**
- Mortgage company: **"Make your One Day – Today"**
- Hyundai: **"Drive Your Way"**
- Harpic: **"What does your loo say about you?"**
- O2: **"The World Revolves Around You"**
- Hugo Fragance: **"Your Fragrance – Your Rules"**
- City & Guilds web site: **"therealyou.com"**

Since the 1950's, before we all had houses stacked out with consumer durables to make our homes safer, trendy, the envy of our neighbours – and to feed the rich, other needs have moved on to the top of the hierarchy.

In the 1970's, two more levels were added to the top of the hierarchy, after 'esteem needs' (4) and before 'self-actualisation' (5 moves to 7). These were generally recognised as:

5. Aesthetic needs – appreciation and search for beauty, balance, form, etc.

6. Cognitive needs – knowledge, meaning, etc.

Not many people in the West could deny that we now live in a culture of celebrity; a social system where the trappings of wealth and fame increase people's self-esteem and motivation to 'do better'. 'The cult of me', that of celebrity worship, is central to many motivators in Western culture. People who self-actualise in a public way are given special status, whether this is through politics, royalty, movie fame or reality TV. Everyone, it seems, wants their fifteen minutes of fame. Our celebrity culture provides one of the motivations for Capitalism: upward mobility through a meritocracy.

But this type of self-centred, self-actualisation is one peculiar to the West. A close look reveals that this particularly Western cultural model is missing important elements for those who believe life on earth might actually have a purpose. It is one of the models at the heart of a dangerous materialistic creed that has produced a 'Me First' culture driven by ego, greed and desire. It has resulted in a cultural philosophy hell-bent on self-annihilation. Stopping Maslow's Hierarchy at 'self-actualisation' reveals the extent of our shallow ambitions for ourselves.

In a moment I am going to reveal some other levels, but what seems to stop people evolving at 'self-actualisation' is one very important question:

"Are we related to something beyond our limited ego sense, something bigger than ourselves, something infinite - or not?"

In other more spiritual cultures the highest attainment of the evolved human is in the service of others. We could call this 'transcendence actualisation' – 'I can't be me unless you can be you!'

This means recognising that on one level whatever I do to you, or you do to me – we also do to ourselves. We are all caught up in the 'circle of life'. This is reflected to a by an addition in the 1990's of another need placed at the top of the hierarchy:

8. Transcendence needs – helping others to achieve self-actualization.

So the whole model from the bottom-up looks like this:

8. Transcendence needs
7. Self-actualisation needs
6. Cognitive needs
5. Aesthetic needs
4. Esteem needs
3. Social needs
2. Safety needs
1. Basic physiological needs

This is a sign that new consciousness is dawning on some members of Western culture. It is a recognition that compassion for others and co-operation may be more important than competition, and that consideration for others is an essential part of sharing a planet.

Some of us are transcending into this realisation of 'mutual survival' where 'what I do to you, I do to myself' because we are all part of one thing. Unfortunately, many people not evolving into this realisation are very busy wrecking the environment for all of us.

If you believe that life has a purpose, that we are here in the universe for a reason then we can add even more layers to the derived Maslow model:

9. Species Actualisation – discovering and working towards all human evolution.
10. Planetary Actualisation – humans working together with the nature on this planet to evolve as one.
11. Universal Actualisation – humans working together with the natural universe to evolve as one.
12. 'God' Actualisation – the actualisation of whatever forces hold this miraculous universe together.
Unfortunately most of humanity is still caught up in the first five levels of Maslow's Hierarchy. It is my belief that humans are just beginning the process of coming into their potential. I see many people as on this journey, despite the best efforts of the social system we have trying to turn us into slaves for a money system.

But the clock is ticking and Nature is just starting to have her say.

Paradigms of Philosophy

The world that we believe we live in is fundamental to how we see ourselves, how we place ourselves in the world. There are many different sets of belief here, often called paradigms. Paradigms change, like the impact of Galileo's work on disproving the flat-earth theory or Copernicus's heresy that the Earth moves round the Sun. These new ideas met a great deal of resistance from existing philosophy but eventually gave rise to a changed perception of the world we live in.

We live now in a time of 'paradigm shift' which creates fundamental changes in our assumptions about the world. For example, our physical sciences have discovered that the whole universe is made of energy. But in the new fields of quantum reality Western medical science is lagging behind in a world of drugs and surgery (although there are many vested interests at work here).

How we perceive the world is central to how we perceive our role in it. There are different perceptions of the world at work speaking incompatible languages. These paradigms have deep roots in our philosophy. Here are three paradigms formative to Western social culture:

Paradigm 1: The Mechanistic View

This paradigm can be traced back to Descartes and other scientists such as Sir Isaac Newton. *The universe is a vast machine and we are all cogs, all with our part to play in its function'.*

The healthy body in a clockwork universe is a well made clock and if it goes wrong we simply take it apart and tinker with the insides until it goes again'.

Rene Descartes (1596 - 1650) was a central influence on the 17th century revolution that began modern science and philosophy. His 'Method of Doubt' was published in 1637:

"I resolved to reject as false everything in which I could imagine the least doubt, in order to see if there afterwards remained anything that was entirely indubitable".

The philosophy of 'Cartesian Dualism' became part of our science, where the mind and the body are seen as essentially separate. The 'self', the conscious being that is 'me' was seen as essentially non-physical. Misguidedly (it was not Descartes intention) this philosophy contributed to the mechanistic and rational philosophy of the universe adopted by our culture. Descartes was one of the first people to suggest that phenomena could be understood by breaking them down into constituent parts and examining each minutely. His view of the human body as a machine functioning within a mechanistic universe took prevalence within the 'Age of Reason'.

Paradigm 2: The Anthropomorphic View

This paradigm is central to the philosophy of Darwinism and others who helped set humans as 'apart and above', or at the head of other life forms. Humanity is the supposed crown of creation, we are created to lord it over every other creature as 'head of the food chain', the Big Ego.

"Let us make mankind . . . rule over the fish in the sea and the birds in the sky, over the livestock and all the wild animals, and over all the creatures that move along the ground,"

God in Genesis 1:26.

The planet is ours to dominate and exploit to our own demands. We must conquer every mountain and battle against disease. We are the most evolved and dominant species in a process of natural selection. We exist for no purpose and have just evolved through sheer luck. In this world our media fantasy industries create amusing stories for us where pigs and fish can talk human to entertain us. Animals are anthropomorphised through culture to have the same needs, desires and dreams as humans. The animals, forests, oceans and environment around us exist purely for our convenience. This paradigm is human self-centred and exploitative to the environment and to ourselves. There are many of people whose whole belief systems are still based within the above paradigms.

Paradigm 3: The Gaian View (an emerging, integrative paradigm)

This paradigm started with Einstein and the science of energy. Its inception combines an age when we saw the first images of the Earth as a whole entity from space. James Lovelock and his search for life on Mars is a central figure in its development through his identification of the Gaia Hypothesis regarding Earth.

This planet we inhabit is a self-balancing, homeostatic system similar to our own as single biological entities. It still maintains the optimum conditions for life (apparently despite our best efforts to pollute it). Our bodies are a miracle of biology, constantly flexible and adaptive but easy to harm. '*Anything we do to it or each other, we do to ourselves as we are part of the same 'web' or 'circle' of life.*' We are part of an evolving cycle of life, a happening miracle. Ourselves, and the environment in which we live are inseparable. Our bodies are a self healing mechanism given the right environment.

Once again, much of our society seems stuck in the earth-abusing first and second paradigms. Those of us who see that everything is connected seem to be speaking a different language. The values associated with the first two paradigms and a perception of Gaia seem utterly opposed.

Eco Philosophy

I was lucky enough to study art and design at Dartington College in Devon, UK. This was a place founded on spiritual values. A Bengali mystic poet called Rabindranath Tagore had been 'adopted' by the owners of Dartington Hall, the Elmhirsts. He became the first non-European to win the Nobel Prize in Literature in 1913. Sometimes referred to as "The Bard of Bengal", Tagore's poetry was viewed as spiritual and mercurial. Tagore was knighted by the ruling British Government in 1915, but within a few years he resigned the honour as a protest against British policies in India. An artist and a rebel, as you might imagine he was soon an influence on me.

"*I slept and dreamt that life was joy. I awoke and saw that life was service. I acted and behold, service was joy.*"

Dartington Hall and College became a place to study art, music and theatre based on spiritual values and when I attended even had its own 'Philosopher in Residence' called Henryk Skolomowski. This was in the 1980's and was my first exposure to the philosophy of ecology, or as he called it in his book, **'Eco Philosophy'**.

We are in a time when our personal and cultural, spiritual and material values are negatively influencing our ability to solve our problems because they are imbalanced. Henryk Skolomowski, in his book, **Eco-Philosophy**, explains that on a molecular level human beings are 'complex fields of force', which also react to their environment as 'complex fields of force'. Quantum physics now endorses this view.

On a molecular level he draws no clear delineation between us and our environment. Skolimowski says that many of our present problems have come about through an elevation of 'knowledge over values', resulting in a general philosophy that regards our environment as something to be conquered rather than cherished.

His book proposes an improved balance of knowledge and values as a means of development, both personal and social, which he calls 'The New Imperative', as opposed to the present day philosophy at the core of our values system.

The table below shows the values of 'Eco Philosophy verses Present Philosophy', from his book. It shows how utterly opposed are the values systems.

PRESENT PHILOSOPHY	ECO-PHILOSOPHY
Pursuing information	Pursuing wisdom
Environmentally and ecologically oblivious	Environmentally and ecologically conscious
Related to the economics of material progress	Related to the economics of the quality of life
Politically indifferent	Politically aware
Socially unconcerned	Socially concerned
Mute about individual responsibility	Vocal about individual responsibility
Intolerant to transphysical	Tolerant to transphysical

phenomena	phenomena
Health mindless	Health mindful
Language orientated	Life orientated
'Objective' (detached)	Committed
Spiritually dead	Spiritually alive
Piecemeal (analytical)	Comprehensive

The values associated with 'present philosophy' and the first and second paradigms as described above are preventing our society from evolving into something wholesome. Although many of us are 'waking up', the social structures we have are controlled by people of extremely limited vision.

It is not enough to just 'change ourselves' or simply 'become the change we wish to see in the world'. We also need to resist at every level the impositions of unevolved people making laws and creating conditions that severly limit our choices to evolve as we might wish to, otherwise we wake up to polluted water and air along with climate catastrophe and slide down the snake to face our basic needs again.

Far be it from me to actually answer the question posed by the heading of this section 'What are Human Beings For?' I could say what I believe my life is for – *'to help others evolve through art'* – I could say that I believe that awake human beings 'in consciousness' are an example of the universe experiencing itself and you might not even know what I mean, let alone agree. What concerns me is the many options being systematically removed, through legislation, from the 'possibilities' available for the amazing phenomenon of humans. It just has to stop!

The term glass ceiling has been traditionally used to describe an unacknowledged barrier to advancement in a profession, especially affecting women and members of minorities. I want to use it here to describe the barrier to evolution that stops with Maslow's 'self-actualisation' and the second paradigm of anthropomorphism as described above – leaving people stranded in a physical, unconnected and spiritually dead universe; a sort of 'spiritual glass ceiling'.

It leaves people as hungry ghosts, doing their best to act out the story of success as told to them over and over. Indigenous American and other people have a concept for this state which they call 'Wetiko'.

Wetiko

From an online article by By Alnoor Ladha & Martin Kirk

"Many spiritual traditions, including Buddhism, Sufism (the mystical branch of Islam), Taoism, Gnosticism, as well as many Indigenous cultures, have long understood the mind-based nature of creation. These world views have at their core a recognition of the power of thought-forms to determine the course of physical events.

Various First Nations traditions of North America have specific and long established lore relating to cannibalism and a term for the thought-form that causes it: wetiko. We believe understanding this offers a powerful way of understanding the deepest roots of our current global polycrisis.

Wetiko is an Algonquin word for a cannibalistic spirit that is driven by greed, excess, and selfish consumption. It deludes its host into believing that cannibalizing the life-force of others (others in the broad sense, including animals and other forms of Gaian life) is a logical and morally upright way to live.

Wetiko short-circuits the individual's ability to see itself as an enmeshed and interdependent part of a balanced environment and raises the self-serving ego to supremacy. It is this false separation of self from nature that makes this cannibalism, rather than simple murder. It allows—indeed commands—the infected entity to consume far more than it needs in a blind, murderous daze of self-aggrandizement. Author Paul Levy, in an attempt to find language accessible for Western audiences, describes it as 'malignant egophrenia'—the ego unchained from reason and limits, acting with the malevolent logic of the cancer cell. We will use the term wetiko as it is the original, and reminds us of the wisdom to be found in Indigenous cultures, for those who have the ears to hear.

Wetiko can describe both the infection and the body infected; a person can be infected by wetiko or, in cases where the infection is very advanced, can personify the disease: 'a wetiko.' This holds true for cultures and systems; all can be described as being wetiko if they routinely manifest these traits.

When Western anthropologists first started to study wetiko, they believed it to be only a disease of the individual and a literal form of flesh-eating cannibalism. On both counts, as discussed, their understanding was, if not wrong, certainly limited. They did, however, accurately isolate two traits that are relevant for thinking about cultures:

> (1) the initial act, even when driven by necessity, creates a residual, unnatural desire for more; and

> (2) the host carrier, which they called the 'victim,' ended up with an 'icy heart'— i.e., their ability for empathy and compassion was amputated.

The reader can probably already sense from the two traits mentioned above the wetiko nature of modern capitalism. Its insatiable hunger for finite resources; its disregard for the pain of groups and cultures it consumes; its belief in consumption as savior; its overriding obsession with its own material growth; and its viral spread across the surface of the planet. It is wholly accurate to describe neoliberal capitalism as cannibalizing life on this planet. It is not the only truth—capitalism has also facilitated an explosion of human life and ingenuity—but when taken as a whole, capitalism is certainly eating through the life-force of this planet in service of its own growth...

In other words, any system that is sufficiently infected by wetiko logic will reward cannibalistic behavior. Or, in Jack Forbes' evocative language, "

Those who squirm upwards [in a wetiko system] are, or become, wetiko, and they only perpetuate the system of corruption or oppression. Thus the communist leaders in the Soviet Union under Stalin were at least as vicious, deceitful and exploitative as their czarist predecessors. They obtained 'power' without changing their wetiko culture."

This ensures that the essential logic of cultures spreads down through generations as well as across them. And it explains why they self-organize resources to maintain a high degree of continuity in distributions of power, when those distributions efficiently serve their survival and growth. When this continuity is interrupted or broken, revolutions occur and the system is put under threat.

However, as the above quote suggests, the disruption must happen at the right level. Merely trading one wetiko for another at the top of an otherwise unchanged wetiko infrastructure (as in the case of Stalin replacing the czars or, more contemporarily, [Trump replacing] Obama replacing Bush) is largely pointless. At best, it might result in the softening of the cruelest edges of a wetiko machine. At worse, it does nothing except distract us from seeing the true infection.

The question, then, for anyone interested in excising the wetiko infection from a culture is, where is it? In one respect, because it is a psychic phenomenon that lives in potential in all of us, it is non-local. But this, though ultimately important to understand, is not the whole truth. It is also true that there is a conceptual place where the most powerful wetiko logic is held, and that, at least in theory, makes it vulnerable.

In the same way that a colony of bees will instinctively house its queen in the deepest chambers of the hive, so a complex adaptive system buries its most important operating logic furthest from the forces that can challenge them. This means two things: first, it means siting the logic in the deep rules that govern the whole. Not just this national economy or that, this government or that, but the mother system—the global operating system. And second, it means making these rules feel as intractable and inevitable as possible.

So what is this deep logic of the global operating system?

It comes in two parts. First, there is the ultimate purpose, which we might call the Prime Directive, which is to **increase capital**.

We often dress this up in a narrative that says capital generation is not the end but the means, the engine of progress. This makes the idea of dethroning it feel dangerous and even contrary to common sense. But the truth is, we have created a system that artificially treats money as sacred. At this point in capitalism's history, life is controlled by, more than it controls, the forces of capital. The clue is really in the name. But if you need further proof, look no further than how we define and measure progress: GDP [& GNP].

Then, there is the logic for how we, the living components of this system, should behave, which we would summarize with the following epithet:

'*Selfishness is rational and rationality is everything; therefore selfishness is everything.*'

This dictates that if we all prioritize ourselves and maximize our own material wealth, an invisible hand will create an equilibrium state and life everywhere will be made better. We are pitted against each other in a form of distributed fascism where we cocoon ourselves in the immediate problems of our own circumstances and consume what we can. We then couch this behavior in the benign language of family matters, national interests, job creation, GDP growth, and other upstanding endeavors.

Put these two parts of the puzzle together and it's easy to see why the banker who generates excess capital receives vast rewards and is labelled 'productive' and 'successful,' almost regardless of the damage s/he causes. Those who are less 'successful' at producing excess capital, meanwhile, are rewarded far less, regardless of the life-affirming good they may be doing. Nurses, mothers, teachers, journalists, activists, scientists—all receive far less reward because they are less efficient at obeying the Prime Directive and may even be countermanding the 'self-interest' operating principle. And as for those who are actually poor—well, they are effortlessly labelled not just as practical but also moral failures.

This infection is so far advanced that the system now requires exponential capital growth. The World Bank tells us that we have to grow the global economy by at least 3 percent per year to avoid recession. Let's think about what this means. Global GDP in 2014 (the last full year of data) was roughly USD $78 trillion. We grew that pie by 2.4% in 2015, which resulted in the commodification and subsequent consumption of roughly another $2 trillion in human labour and natural resources. That's roughly the size of the entire global economy in 1970. It took us from the dawn of civilization to 1970 to reach $2 trillion in global GDP, and now we need that just in the differential so the entire house of cards doesn't crumble. In order to achieve this rate of growth year-on-year, we are destroying our planet, ensuring mass species extinction, and displacing millions of our brothers and sisters (who we commonly refer to as 'poor people') from around the world. So when people tell us that the market knows best, or technology will save us, or philanthrocapitalism will redistribute opportunities (pace Bill Gates), we have to understand that all of these seemingly common sense truisms are embedded in a broader operating system, a wetikonomy, with all that that means. And the more they are presented as 'unchangeable,' the more often we're told, 'there is no alternative,' the more we should question. There is actually a beautiful irony in the fact that, when we know what we're up against, such statements are our signposts for where to look."

By Alnoor Ladha, Martin Kirk

http://www.kosmosjournal.org/article/seeing-wetiko-on-capitalism-mind-viruses-and-antidotes-for-a-world-in-transition/

The Wisdom of Indigenous people

"In the 1990s an unusual encounter took place in the Ecuadorian Amazon. In plant rituals, shamans of the Achuar, a tribe living in pristine forest that had never been in touch with Western civilization, received the warning that the 'white man' would try to invade their lands, cut down the forest and exploit the resources. Deeply shaken, they called out to the Spirits for help. Soon after white people did approach them, coming to them however with supportive intentions – a group of activists from the United States, searching for ways to protect Indigenous Peoples from the oil industry. The Westerners found a deeply interconnected tribal society living in profound symbiosis with the Earth. Seeing the bulldozers coming closer and closer, they asked the Elders of the tribe how they could survive. Their answer was surprising and straightforward: "Don't try to help us here. Go back to your own culture and change the dream of the modern world! It is because of this dream that we are perishing."

Martin Winiecki

The Kogi

I am fascinated by what is happening on this earth at the moment with Indigenous Peoples. Possibly they are the only civilised races living on the planet but are being hounded out of their sustainable relationships with the Earth by people with a vested interest in exploiting it for money. This has now been going on for thousands of years, since before illegal immigrants crushed their opposition in North America with smallpox infested blankets as gifts.

"The Great Lie is that this is civilisation. It is not civilised. It has been literally the most bloodthirsty, brutalising system ever imposed on this planet. This is not civilisation, this is the Great Lie. Or if it does represent civilisation and that is truly what civilisation is, then the Great Lie is that civilisation is good for us."

John Trudell

I read of the Lakota Indians of North America, driven from their ancestral lands so that people can build things there. My favourite indigenous tribe are the Kayapo, who have interested me ever since reading Sting's book about them over 30 years ago. Like other tribes in the Amazon they are driven from their forests by loggers, their lands raped and ruined by developers in order to build dams to power cities or extract oil. If anything their situation is now worse then when Sting bought them to our attention by living with the tribe. The Masai Tribe, beautiful people living in tune with the harshest of environments, legislated off their ancestral land, the Masai Mara, and banned from hunting so that it can be exploited for tourism and Land Rover adverts. The Aboriginal people of Australia, alive with incredible stories of nature and belonging, singing their reality into being, but driven from sustainable lifestyles in tune with their lands by a culture of greed and consumerism which is divorced from nature.

It seems to me that the way we treat our indigenous peoples on this earth is a metaphor for the way we treat nature itself. So when the rarely seen Kogi Indians came down from their High Sierra retreat in the mountains of Colombia to make a movie about how 'little brother' is destroying the Earth, I wanted to watch it. This is an excerpt of how the movie is described on the Aluna website:

"ALUNA is made by and with the KOGI, a genuine lost civilization hidden on an isolated triangular pyramid mountain in the Sierra Nevada de Santa Marta, Colombia, nearly five miles high, on the Colombian-Caribbean coast. The Kogi say that without thought, nothing could exist.

This is a problem, because we are not just plundering the world, we are dumbing it down, destroying both the physical structure and the thought underpinning existence. The Kogi believe that they live in order to care for the world and keep its natural order functioning, but they recognized some years ago that this task was being made impossible by our mining and deforestation. In 1990 they emerged to work with Alan Ereira, making a 90-minute film for BBC1 in which they dramatically warned of our need to change course. Then they withdrew again..."

Ostensibly Aluna is a story of a few members of the tribe collecting 400 km of gold thread from England, and then returning to Colombia to walk across their ruined lands, showing the devastation to the camera whilst also connecting places with the thread in an attempt to demonstrate to 'little brother' that all things are connected.

For example, in the foothills of the High Sierra, where the land meets the sea the people who have taken the ancestral lands from the Kogis have built roads, cutting off lagoons from the sea and stopping the natural flow. To these people there is no link between what happens at the top of the Sierra Nevada de Santa Marta and the lagoons far below. The Kogi Indians assert that if the land were a human being, what has happened is the equivalent of cutting off its ability to cycle its wastes. As one of them says in a moment of blinding lucidity: *"How would you like it if I stuck a cork up your arse."*

Ecology scientists agree that the Kogi are right – their ecosystems at the top of the mountains are being seriously damaged through unconsidered development below.

Of course from my point of view, the Kogi people are right on the button with their accusations that 'little brother' is destroying the planet. There are many people out here in the First World who feel the same way they do. Its just that we don't know how to stop the people responsible because they are all 'government sponsored'.

It is completely unfair to compare a movie like Aluna with the highest grossing eco-movie ever, Avatar, which has an improbably large budget, but there is a world of difference in the approach. Some people criticise Avatar on the basis that it is ecology reduced to spectacle, drama and conflict and that people don't even realise that it is a metaphor about our own planet and culture, hence it is ineffective in changing people's motivations away from 'Unobtanium' – the movie's metaphor for eco-damaging self-interest and profit.

Aluna has more in common with the movie 'Age of Stupid'. As such it is a movie of 'finger pointing greenyism' which is mostly preaching to the converted like myself, and making other people feel guilty for something they do not believe that they have much power over – the irreversible damaging of the present ecosystems on earth in the pursuit of money.

In the context of the culture of lies inhabited by little brother, unfortunately the movie Aluna is an innocent whose voice will not be much heeded in a culture that values superficiality and sensationalism. The problem is not so much that people do not realise that their actions have damaging consequences to our planet. I think many people know this but choose to deny it. Because they are afraid, they just don't want to know.

"Man is full if he is in tune with the universe; if he is not in tune with the universe then he is empty, utterly empty. And out of that emptiness comes greed. Greed is to fill it: by money, by houses, by furniture, by friends, by lovers – by anything, because one cannot live as emptiness. It is horrifying, it is a ghost life. If you are empty and there is nothing inside you, it is impossible to live."

Osho, Beyond Psychology, Talk #26

They are trapped and driven as hungry ghosts, wanting all sorts of things without which they can never be complete. I think that little brother and its society has serious problems. We simply choose not to see things that we don't want to. We edit reality to suit ourselves. We would sooner lie to ourselves than see the effects of our actions.

Eckart Tolle believes: *"The pollution of the planet is only an outward reflection of an inner psychic pollution; millions of unconscious individuals not taking responsibility for their inner space."*

As the horror of what humans are doing to their planet becomes more evident – the denial becomes stronger. We are at the stage now where many people simply ignore all information that does not validate their existing ideology. We all seem to live in filter bubbles. This has become so extreme that in Japan half a million people are named 'hikikomori' –

so withdrawn into virtual worlds that they can no longer be reached by those around them!

2. THE PURPOSE OF GOVERNMENT

Society and the Individual

One of the reasons we need government is to find a balance between the needs of the individual and that of the society within which that individual is a part. Arthur Koestler in ' *The Act of Creation* 'describes the need to fit in, to conform, as a 'participatory tendency' within a system. He writes that this is a polarity of attitude, the other end of the scale being a 'self assertive tendency'.

"The polarity between the self asserting and participatory tendencies turns out to be a particular instance of a general phenomenon: namely that every member of a living organism or social body has the dual attributes of 'wholeness' and 'partness'. It acts as an autonomous, self-governing whole on its own subordinate parts on the lower levels of the organic or social hierarchy; but is subservient to the co-ordinating centre on the next higher level".

Koestler relates these polarities to the extremes of centrifugal and centripetal force, *"The former asserting the parts interdependence, autonomy and individuality, the second keeping it in place as a dependant part in the whole".* This balance or 'synergy' of part and whole defines not only our role as individuals in a society, but is central to many issues affecting us in a modern world.

One parallel is cancer. When a cell forgets its part in the whole organ or body and starts replicating for itself, its synergy has gone. The participatory tendency is lost and it becomes completely self assertive and damages the host body. No wonder it is a disease of the Western world and very much on the increase in our synergy-less society.

The point of government is that it is meant to manage this process of synergy, allowing us freedom and self-expression, the ability to lead, to exercise responsibilty, to discover – but also making rules so that we can all live reasonably with each other in the larger body of society. Anything more than this is an intrusion.

"Our appreciation of what a good life could be is limited by vested interests such as those of the dominant commercial and political system. This system equates the good life with factors like limitless economic growth, consumption, accumulation of monetary wealth and processed convenience foods.

This means that, when confronted by the need to change these assumptions, people feel aggrieved that they are being required to give up the good life. What is actually needed is to reframe the essence of the good life in a new system of living. Evidence is accumulating that moves toward greater resilience actually enhance our experience of the good life. They are not opposing goals if tackled in the right way."

Anthony Hodgson

Unfortunately our representative system of government has grown into an oligarchy. It now intrudes into every level of life and creates rules that benefit only a privileged minority. It has become the cancer, its actions leading to the devastation of the all the qualities that life needs to survive, in the name of 'Economic Growth', presently the dominant myth in our culture. It assumes that there is little need to change the way we live. 'Economic Growth' is regarded as essential for our prosperity as individuals but in reality serves only a few. The richest eight people in the world now own as much as half of the world's population. The central tenet in this myth is that in order to grow as individuals, as a society, even as a race, we have to focus on making money.

However to live this myth we are spending three planets when we only have one, and using the limited resources of our little planet as if it were an infinite income. We are damaging the land, air and oceans and even wiping out the very cultures, like the Kogi, who could help to show us how to live within limits.

Government Protects?

One reason Governments are supposedly here is to protect us from conflict, externally or internally, and to provide law and order in a set of rules, or laws. In actuality the US and the UK are instigators of conflict. The US are militarily dominant and aggressive to say the least. I mean, for how many decades must the United States attack and occupy oil-rich countries before you realise who the real terrorists are? In 2016 the American government, led by Nobel Peace Prize winner President Obama, was responsible for dropping 26,171 bombs. That's 3 bombs an hour, 24 hours a day, all year. They were dropped on Syria, Iraq, Afghanistan, Libya, Yemen, Somalia and Pakistan.

Trump's ban on Muslim immigrants includes five of these countries, plus Iran and Sudan whose terrorists don't seem to have killed any Americans on American soil. Records show American 'deaths by terrorism' between 1975 and 2015 are attributed to: Saudi Arabia: 2,369, United Arab Emirates: 314, Egypt: 162 and Lebanon: 159.

Just to put this into perspective, other American deaths are attributed, averaging over the same time period to: armed toddlers: 840, lightning: 1240, lawnmowers: 2760, hit by bus: 10,560, falling out of bed: 29,480, shot by another American: 469,480. Incidentally, 20,000 people in this world die every day from poverty – over the same time frame, that's 7,300000 per year, about 292 million over the same 40 years.

The outgoing President signed into law the 2017 National Defense Authorisation Act, giving $611,000,000,000 (that's billion – I just wanted to see it in numbers) for military spending in one year. Since 9/11 the US has spent nearly £5 trillion on wars – that's $5,000,000,000,000. Trump has added 9% on top of this.

The reasons for these wars are obvious. The same as all wars; the extension of resources through armed conflict and aggression, whatever the 'excuse'. In the year 2000 the countries listed as without centralised 'Rothschild Banks' were Afghanistan, Iraq, Sudan, Libya, Cuba, North Korea, Iran and Syria. By 2003 Afghanistan and Iraq were 'off this list', and by 2016 so were Sudan and Libya. Cuba is 'under peaceful invasion' by the US, leaving just North Korea, Iran and Syria to complete the Monopoly Board of Global Financial Control. Watch this space!

The UK is the second biggest biggest arms dealer on the planet. Its population's investment policies and pensions are dependant on 'using up' the arms every 15 years or so in made-up conflicts to profit the banks and their shareholders.

For example the British Government are arms dealers for United Arab Emirates to fuel the Saudi leveling of Yemen. UK local government employees and councils are forced by law to invest their pension funds in UAE and the oil corporations, hence creating profit for their retirements from the ethnic cleansing of Palestinians on the West Bank.

Britain's arms deals fuel deadly conflicts in the Middle East. Since 2010 Britain has sold arms to 39 of the 51 countries ranked "not free" on the Freedom House "Freedom in the World" report, and 22 of the 30 countries on the UK Government's own human rights watch list. A full two-thirds of UK weapons over this period were sold to Middle Eastern countries, where instability has fed into increased risk of terror threats to Britain and across the West. Boat loads of Syrians fleeing the conflict and their ruined homes to Europe do so because of British arms.

We are ruled by an elite group of psychopaths who run the banks that control the government and media. They fund both sides of war for profit and they manufacture the consent of the public through the propaganda of the media and distract people with shiny bling and celebrity gossip.

They hide the truth, they distract, they lie and control.

Government Fosters Wellbeing?

Apart from 'protecting their people' from others and themselves, another important function of government was to provide for their wellbeing – to protect them from external events which might affect them. Unfortunately this seems to have been lost as government is now, and often highly connected to, the heart of 'economics' – a vast industrial machine built to exploit the earth's resources and turn them into money for a few priviledged people who support the government from behind the scenes.

We have reached a time now, when individual people, sick of (and often from) the continual raping of their environment for financial profit, are coming forwards as 'protectors'. Protectors of water, air, sunlight, wildlife, environments – from the giant harvesting machine sponsored by government's addiction to the madness of 'economics'.

They are often treated as scum and abused by government interdict, by the very forces that are meant to protect them. Recent events at an oil pipeline in Dakota provide clear examples. It is my belief that the 'black snake' of oil being halted by a collective of Indigenous American Tribes (and veterans) may be a seminal event in the history of mankind's relationship with the planet. Water is life indeed and those at Oceti Sakowin camp have stood up to extreme abuse, not to mention the dead of winter, to show people a way forward.

Under the guise of protection from 'terrorism', puppet governments have now bought in swingeing laws, such as 'The Investigatory Powers Act' in the UK. This allows the government and their agents to access any information they require, even hacking personal computers and phones in an attempt to forestall any objectors to their plans and those of their overlords. Whistleblowers like Edward Snowden or Julian Assange, who expose the truth of what is going on are harangued on trumped-up charges that diminish them in the public eye – hence marginalising their influence.

One thing is increasingly certain, an industrial infrastructure is no longer compatible with the conditions for healthy life on Earth. If this is to continue the global political and economic structures we have need to be dismantled. This process is something that can no longer be trusted to governments with any capitalist interest. Economic development is leading us towards global ecological, economic and social collapse from environmental destruction and climate change.

"We might summarize our present human situation by the simple statement... the glory of the human has become the desolation of the Earth and now the desolation of the Earth is becoming the destiny of the human.

From here on, the primary judgment of all human institutions, professions, programs and activities will be determined by the extent to which they inhibit, ignore, or foster a mutually-enhancing human/Earth relationship."

Thomas Berry

Government is Honest?

As an anarchist I like to be non-party political. As Lierre Keith of Deep Green Resistance says: *"The task of an activist is not to navigate systems of oppressive power with as much personal integrity as possible, it is to dismantle these systems."* But there is one member of UK parliament for whom I have a great deal of respect, Caroline Lucas, the only MP for the Green Party.

Her book, '*Honourable Friends, Parliament and the Fight for Change*' is a complete eye-opener to the machinations of Parliament in the UK. One of the few people since Guy Fawkes to enter Parliament with honest intentions, Caroline Lucas is on the forefront of bringing ideas about desperately needed reform to Parliament. As events since her book was published have revealed, that particular branch swings ever more frustratingly out of reach as corporate control is now at the heart of our supposedly democratic government. Government as we have it is un-reformable. It is my opinion that our sovereignty as a nation has already been sold.

"Sovereignty is about how we as individuals, communities and as nations govern ourselves, what we retain as our essential rights; and where we pool sovereignty so that we can, working together, be stronger than our individual parts... the fundamental problem with Parliament is that those within it believe they are sovereign; they are the ultimate source of power and authority; and they are then tempted to misude it, selling it to sectional interests, lobbyists, big business and the rest. "

The threat of terrorism has been used to remove many of our fundamental rights as citizens.

"In the last few years, we have lost the right to silence; the right to be tried in open court, not behind closed doors; the right to see the evidence being used against you and to cross-examine witnesses; and even the oldest of them all, habeus corpus, has been compromised. Under the Terrorism Prevention and Investigation Measures Act you can be confined to your own house, your visitors controlled and your phone calls restricted...it is exactly this slow, drip-by-drip erosion of our liberties that is so dangerous."

Law after law is passed that undermine essential freedoms in favour of corporate control, hidden under the guise of 'preventing terrorism' or 'harmonisation'. Donnachadh McCarthy, author of '*The Prostitute State: How Britain's Democracy Has Been Bought*' summarises the effects some of those underway at present:

- Turning Britain into an even greater immoral thieving tax-haven than we already are. They would give away billions to the rich 1% owned corporations by abolishing Corporation Tax. This will be funded by further massive slashing of public services and the placing all of remaining tax burden on employees. This would be a disaster for all working people across Europe, as it would force their governments to do the same or face loss of all their corporations HQs to the UK.

- They are abolishing what remains of social housing in the UK.

- They are seeking to abolish whole swathes of environmental health protections.

- They are ensuring fossil fuel and nuclear corporations get massive help from taxpayers.

- They want to abolish totally the NHS and have a 100% privatised NHS.

- They want to slash help for the poor in the UK and slash international development aid for the poorest in the world.

- They want "free trade" treaties that abolish the right of the UKs elected government to implement any future environmental regulations and make illegal for the elected UK government to implement any nationalisations of key industries like health or railways or post-office.

- They want to abolish all our international human rights treaty protections.

- They want to destroy what remains of the trade unions and workers rights.

- They want to slash the number of elected MPs, whilst they are packing the House of Lords with hundreds of more right wing corporate donors.

- They are attacking the right to vote by bringing in new requirements for US style voter ID laws and more difficult voter registration laws that mean hundreds of thousands of poorer voters are falling off the voter rolls.

- They are facilitating Murdoch's disastrous fascist monopoly on our prostituted media by letting him take over all of Sky, potentially turning it into another Fox News, which would take a ball and chain to what remains of our battered prostituted democracy and he has also taken over another chain of UK radio stations, the TalkSport chain.

Representative Democracy?

In April 1938, President Franklin Roosevelt sent the US Congress the following warning: *"The liberty of a democracy is not safe if the people tolerate the growth of private power to a point where it becomes stronger than their democratic state itself. That, in its essence, is fascism."*

This United Kingdom has long ceased to be united or even a democracy. One definition of **democracy** is: *'a government in which the supreme power is vested in the people and exercised by them directly or indirectly through a system of representation'.*

The supreme power in the representative system we have is invested in just two-thirds of the population because one-third – for whatever reasons is entirely disenfranchised and does not vote. In the UK it is presently exercised by a non-elected prime minister who has appointed a cabinet of people defined by their possession of money.

When the governments that are voted in routinely ignore the will of the people, be that over wars, cuts, or the minutiae of policy, we see modern representative democracy for the sham that it is. Allowing protest only on condition that it will never present a challenge to government is part of that same sham.

What can we do when the government itself is the problem? It is so self-referencial that even the intelligent and more fairly representative option of 'proportional representation' fails to be adopted. Whoever you vote for – the government gets in and they work to support a 'Keynesian Free Market Economy', a brand of economics which is contrary to the interests of life itself.

What of more radical options like a 'directly participatory democratic system', where we all vote on issues as they emerge? Such things will never even be heard of from within a system that seeks to ban anything radical, promoting any alternative ideas that challenge the mainstream as a form of terrorism. The concept of participatory democracy will be explored more fully later in this book.

The system we have is presently more like an **oligarchy** – *'a form of government in which all power is vested in a few persons or in a dominant class or clique; government by the few.'* Our elected representatives are in fact, acting in the interests of money and big-business, not of us – the people who put them there.

Some people believe the system to be more like a **plutocracy** – *'a class or group ruling, or exercising power or influence, by virtue of its wealth'*, in which anyone else is a slave serving their interests, otherwise facing arrest or punitive action for non-compliance. Anyone involved in the peaceful protests about fracking will have seen or experienced this for themselves.

I have even heard the system we have defined as a **kleptocracy** – *'a government or state in which those in power exploit national resources and steal from us to increase their own wealth; rule by thieves.'*

As explored earlier – it could also be called a **Wetiocracy**! – *' government pursuing an undefined and unquestioned set of values that consume life for private purpose and profit.'*

Even worse – **pathocracy** – *'a system of government in which individuals with personality disorders (especially psychopathy) occupy positions of power and influence. The result is a totalitarian system characterised by a government turned against its own people.'*

I have seen events in which all of the above are true.

Representative democracy is no longer working for people, it is no longer a representative but a corporate oligarchy. In this age of complexity it is not possible for one person to represent many views. In fact I find pretty much none of my concerns are presently represented in a parliamentary system. Around 64 million people in the UK, represented by just 650 members of parliament leaves 98,461 people per MP; hardly representative!

The false dichotomy of a two-party system reduces discourses down to a tiny ideological platform, both of which support Keynsian Economics at the price of environmental damage. This is nowhere near the complexity that we have in the actual political positions of people.

City-centrist decisions made on local issues are invariably just wrong – especially where I live in a very rural environment! What applies in the city often doesn't work in the country and sometimes local conditions are often not even considered in legislation made centrally.

Our only real alternative is to build self-governance up from a local level to reclaim the powers that we have given to a corrupt, uninformed and out-of-touch government.

When you look at the government we have today do you really feel represented by these people? The whole system of a 'representative democracy' has become a joke. The leaders seem like pantomime villains acting out an entirely predictable script of lining their own nests.

It is a system of representation made for a slave mentality, for people who wish to be governed. It is a nest of tyrants. Far better for people interested in a balanced life of 'freedom and responsibility' is the idea of a more directly participatory democracy in which the people can govern themselves if they choose to.

There are much better options than the anachronism of Parliament we presently have, but it is the system of government itself that is preventing them from even seeing the light of day. A representative democracy is no longer serving its people.

Its time to get rid of the lot of them.

"Obviously I don't vote as I believe democracy is a pointless spectacle where we choose between two indistinguishable political parties, neither of whom represent the people but the interests of the powerful business elites that own the world."

Russell Brand

Caroline Lucas describes the awful inefficiency, the money wasted, the back room deals, the ridiculously out-dated procedures, the downright ignorance and arrogance and the old-boy network. She shows the red tape, the meaningless and time consuming traditions and the insidious corruption inherent in the system. Her book clearly describes the hideously outdated, biased and remote nature of government in the UK.

She exposes many of the absurdities of this uniquely British cross between a serious parliament and a taxpayer-subsidised, champagne-and-canape gentlemen's club (and they are mainly men in suits), such as the antiquated, time-consuming voting procedure of the division bell calling Honourable Members to vote from wherever they happen to be in or around the premises, in eight minutes flat, to be sometimes physically pushed by their party whips into the Aye or No lobbies, there to be manually counted as electronic voting has yet to arrive in the British Parliament, and often having little idea of what they're voting for.

She writes about the blatant unfairness of the Private Members' Bills, which are discussed on Friday afternoons when the Commons is particularly empty, but require the backing of a hundred MPs and are usually 'talked out' (filibustered until they run out of time) if the Government dislikes the proposal. Or the quaint Ruritanian provision of ribbons in the member's cloakroom upon which to hang one's sword. I find it a wonder that she still believes that parliament is actually capable of reform.

She writes about her attempts to reform such an anachronistic institution as 'The Mutha of All Parliaments' which is no longer relevant to the modern world. Such an entrenched institution is beyond reform and it is leading us towards environmental and social breakdown because it is no longer representative of the people and has become an oligarchy. Essentially – this is what they have brought us:

National Debt

"Mainstream media headlines today are focused on Britain's record national debt, which just surpassed £1 trillion, a figure that can only exponentially increase unless the entire mechanism of Government finance is overhauled. The truth however is much worse, factoring in all liabilities including state and public sector pensions, the real national debt is closer to £4.8 trillion, some £78,000 for every person in the UK."

http://www.nationaldebtclock.co.uk/

"As of November 2016, debt held by the public in the United States was $14.3 trillion or about 76% of the previous 12 months of GDP. Intragovernmental holdings stood at $5.4 trillion, giving a combined total gross national debt of $19.8 trillion or about 106% of the previous 12 months of GDP. $6.2 trillion or approximately 45% of the debt held by the public was owned by foreign investors, the largest of which were China and Japan at about $1.25 trillion for China and $1.15 trillion for Japan as of May 2016." (Wikipedia) It is projected to increase and you can see it ticking away at :

http://www.usdebtclock.org/

So in the UK capitalism has, at time of writing, bought a debt of £78,000 for every man, woman and child. In the US every citizen owes $61,335 which works out as $167,000 per taxpayer. Not only has capitalism failed but the socio-economic system of which it is a part continues to rape our planet and systematically destroy the conditions needed for life on earth.

Dedication to Capitalism

Our systems of government are devoted to the manangement of this economic system of extractivism. In fact they have come to be ruled by it. But worldly ambition, material aspiration and 'perpetual economic growth' are not only a formula for environmental destruction but also it seems one for mass-unhappiness.

The mega-rich cause damaging financial crises with wild speculation, get bailed out by taxpayers, then argue that public spending on schools and hospitals should be slashed to meet the resulting deficits - all while many of them fail to pay their legal share of taxes! This austerity-spiral is driving a rapid worldwide increase in inequality.

An email in possession of Wikileaks demonstrates the absolute complicity of money and government in the US. This is from a executive at Citibank's parent company, giving all of the names of President Obama's cabinet a month before his election in 2008. The big banks decide who runs the economy and the country even before the elections take place, because our governments are here to service corporate consumerism.

"Corporations... have now been assigned a human and legal personality and now they are trying to disposses people of their democratic rights, and they are trying to disposses nature of her rights. We are at a watershed for human evolution. We will either defend the rights of people and the earth and for that we will have to dismantle the rights that corporations have assigned to themselves or corporations will in the next three decades destroy this planet in terms of human possibilities."

Vandana Shiva

The Pirates

"Progress in our society is measured by the speed at which we destroy the conditions that sustain life."

George Monbiot

Legendary actor John Cleese was watching the election unfold on American television and observed that; *"It looks as though Trump is assembling the crew for a pirate ship,"* rather than people who will lead the United States. Our governments are set up to plunder the planet for profit and reduce human potential to slavery in the process.

It is the role of 'the pirates' of capitalism to commodify nature. To take from us what is rightfully ours and then sell it back to us for money. Pouring black oil into water so that it is undrinkable, scarce and expensive. Killing the bees with toxic pesticides so that they can be replaced with electronic insect drones, copyrighting nature itself in unbelievable acts of bio-piracy that steal nature's resources directly from us.

The same companies that fill our homes with cancer producing chemicals, provide the toxic treatments that supposedly 'cure' us and government legislation endorses this in support of money. For hundreds of years now, since the beginning of the Industrial Revolution such wealth production at any cost has been celebrated and the industrial champions of the world admired and revered. So now they want our water, our air, our sunlight, our nature and unless we act, they will take it from us for the rewards of money and the status that this brings to a few insecure people. Just 8 billionaires have as much wealth as the poorest half of our planet; wealth they too often use to buy politicians and capture our democracies to keep the whole system going in their favour.

"Unchecked consumerism operates on the premise that others are only instruments to be used and that the environment is a commodity. This attitude fosters unhappiness, selfishness and contempt upon other living beings and upon our environment. People are rarely motivated to change on behalf of something for their future and that of the next generation. They resist the idea of giving up what they enjoy just for the sake of avoiding long-term disastrous effects."

Matthieu Ricard

Pro-business rhetoric rules our governments and this can be seen in the high level of climate-deniers within the UK Conservative government. Caroline Lucas states that: *"71% of Conservative MPs think that human induced climate change is either unproven or 'environmentalist propaganda'"*. This frightening deviation to the norm is precisely because the action needed to slow down the effects of global warming run contrary to the vested interests of business people and 'extractivism' in general. It gets even worse when we look at the American government, who seem to have been chosen on the basis of denying global climate changes.

Government in Denial

Behind the polished smiles & fraudulent oratory the Minister of Energy and Clean Growth, and her Welsh and Scottish counterparts, dispense with the Committee on Climate Change and embrace a Trumpian view of science.

The Government's climate Minister, Claire Perry, wrote to the Chair of the Committee on Climate Change requesting their advice on the implications for the UK of the IPCC's recent 1.5°C report. Albeit three years overdue, a cursory reading of the letter suggests that the Government's reluctance to take climate change seriously may be thawing. Sadly, a few moments reflection dispels any such romantic notion.

The Minister opened her letter[1] with a disingenuous statement that did not bode well. The UK has apparently decoupled its emissions (down by over "40%") from economic growth (up by around 66%). Nonsense. Selective accounting and offshored emissions are the leading lights in this fairy tale performance. Include emissions from aviation and shipping and those associated with our import and exports, and the carbon footprint for UK plc. has barely changed since 1990. This certainly puts a very different complexion on the climate challenge – but not one this government is keen to face.

In penning the letter, Claire Perry & the devolved signatories surgically scythed away the real substance of any review. The CCC is permitted only to comment on the implications of Paris for post 2032 – by when most front benchers will be writing memoirs or fertilising daisies. The offending sentence notes how "Carbon budgets already set in legislation (covering 2018-2032) are out of scope of this request."

The Minister then proceeds to toughen her preference for near-term Party politics over robust analysis and honest debate when, in bold, she orders the 'independent' CCC to inform on "long term" targets, and later in the letter, what needs to be done "by 2050". Nowhere does she acknowledge the IPCC's recent call for drastic reductions in emissions by 2030 if we are to have any chance of meeting our 1.5°C commitment.[2]

But is any of this really unexpected? And perhaps more importantly, why have this government been allowed the space and time to embellish their climate rhetoric whilst forcing through high-carbon fracking, airport expansion and stifling solar pv and onshore wind.

Again I turn to my academic community – where are our voices! This is an existential threat for so many people and species, yet we typically remain silent in the face of political and commercial interests.

In 1967 and as part of academia's efforts to curtail the worse excesses of the Vietnam war, Bertrand Russell established the International War Crimes Tribunal. A half a century later and facing the threats posed by anthropogenic climate change, is it time again for academics to use their research as a platform for speaking out rather than appeasing the status quo?

If so, could this Government's hamstringing of the Committee on Climate Change finally be a call to arms?

[1]https://assets.publishing.service.gov.uk/government/uploads/syste
m/uploads/attachment_data/file/748489/CCC_commission_for_Pari
s_Advice_-_Scot__UK.pdf

[2]http://report.ipcc.ch/sr15/pdf/sr15_spm_final.pdf
This entry was posted in Blog, Uncategorized on October 16, 2018.

Puppet Government

Theresa May's 27-strong cabinet in the UK hardly reflects the diversity of modern Britain: 18 white male millionaires, 7 white female millionaires and two Asian millionaires. The US's new government is even worse in terms of a bias towards a financial perception.

Yet the very basis of consumer capitalism is that we can never have enough. We exist to service our 'economy' by consuming and by being made into 'hungry ghosts' by the corporately controlled mass-media, never satisfied, always yearning for something more. The endless stream of 4,000 visual and auditory messages a day are contrived to make us incomplete. The main political parties tend this machine, as does the majority of our privately owned media.

Almost the entirety of government in the UK and US is populated by people in pursuit of financial wealth, or those who already own huge amounts. These people serve money and the people who possess it. Big money possesses our governments and acts in its own interest. It is what George Monbiot has named 'dark money'.

This political cartoon by Pia Guerra comments on Steve Bannon's influence in Donald Trump's Whitehouse.

Figure 1: Trump cartoon

But the people at the top don't just sit on bundles of money – they own the corporations that generate it. The 10 richest billionaires on the earth are entrepreneurs, investors, businessmen and industrialists. United States currently has the most billionaires amongst the world's top 10 but India is expected to soon overtake the United States to gain more billionaires among the world's top 10 than any other country.

The 2015 Forbes global billionaire list shows a record 1,826 billionaires with an aggregate net worth of $7.05 trillion, up from $6.4 trillion a year ago. The total includes 290 newcomers, 71 of whom hail from China. Youth are on the rise: A record 46 billionaires among the ranks are under age 40.

The people who own our governments also own the banks to which we are all in debt. They own the media we all stream and watch, the pharmaceuticals and 'treatments' that our health services provide. They sponsor the money that provides our national educational provision – mostly now in the interest of business and industry. Through all of these they provide a kind of 'movie' – a set of behavioural norms to which we must adhere to succeed. These stories are told to us over and over again right from the earliest age. Stories in the media, educational curricula, the health services, energy, legislation – all enforcing the same basic life patterns and pressure to conform.

Big business even pays for many positions within the government and civil service through sponsored jobs, where they pay the salary of the person working within the government department – a completely opaque (eg not transparent) practice.

"The combination of lobbying, the erosion of the independence of the civil service and the capture of the political elite by big business has made for a toxic combination...When businesses start funding political parties then its as if one side were handing money to the judge to get the judgement they want".

Caroline Lucas

"In the US, there is basically one party - The Business Party. It has two factions, called Democrats and Republicans, which are somewhat different but carry out variations on the same policies. By and large, I am opposed to these policies. As is most of the population."

Noam Chomsky

Trade Agreements

Trade legislation and agreements give insight into the type of goals that government and corporate interests want to achieve so I have provided some examples.

Codex Alimentarius

A few years ago there was an EU Directive on Herbal Medicine. This was not a trade agreement as such but was named 'Codex Alimentarius', a Latin title presumably contrived to limit the interest of as many people as possible.

New legislation concerning food and health, is often applied under the guise of 'safety' and 'harmonisation', but it is structured to limit our choices and access to natural foods and alternative medicines.

New drugs are becoming hard for the chemical industries to find – not to mention expensive to develop. So why not just patent nature – take what we have away from us using legislation – and then sell it back to us for profit? Hence the birth of biopiracy! After all pirating nature is one way capitalism has worked for years.

Codex Alimentarius is a perfect example of the complicity between politicians and economic and financial powers, industry and state working together for their exclusive mutual benefit and shows how governments are increasingly the lackeys of big business. Codex Alimentarius and the EU Directive has made legislation in Europe that effectively gives control of our foods and supplements, such as herbs, vitamins and 'natural' treatments into the hands of big business to do with as they will. Codex Alimentarius has attained its long-time goal of giving control of vitamins, supplements and food to pharmaceutical corporations - with much reduced dosages in commercially available herbal preparations, rendering them mostly ineffective - and putting the independents out of business.

According to John Hammell, a legislative advocate and the founder of International Advocates for Health Freedom (IAHF):

"... herbs, vitamins, minerals, homeopathic remedies, amino acids and other natural remedies you have taken for granted most of your life will be gone. The name of the game for Codex Alimentarius is to shift all remedies into the prescription category so they can be controlled exclusively by the medical monopoly and its bosses, the major pharmaceutical firms."

TTIP

Another attempt by Big Corporate to take power and absolve themselves of any responsibility was called 'The Transatlantic Trade and Investment Partnership'. From Lee Williams of the Independent; "It was a series of trade negotiations being carried out mostly in secret between the EU and US. As a bi-lateral trade agreement, TTIP is about reducing the regulatory barriers to trade for big business, things like food safety law, environmental legislation, banking regulations and the sovereign powers of individual nations. It is, as John Hilary, Executive Director of campaign group War on Want, said: "An assault on European and US societies by transnational corporations."

Since before TTIP negotiations began, the process has been secretive and undemocratic. This secrecy is on-going, with nearly all information on negotiations coming from leaked documents and Freedom of Information requests. But worryingly, the covert nature of the talks may well be the least of our problems. Here are six other reasons why we should be scared of TTIP, very scared indeed:

1 The NHS

Public services, especially the NHS, are in the firing line. One of the main aims of TTIP is to open up Europe's public health, education and water services to US companies. This could essentially mean the privatisation of the NHS.

2 Food and environmental safety

TTIP's 'regulatory convergence' agenda will seek to bring EU standards on food safety and the environment closer to those of the US. But US regulations are much less strict, with 70 per cent of all processed foods sold in US supermarkets now containing genetically modified ingredients. By contrast, the EU allows virtually no GM foods. The US also has far laxer restrictions on the use of pesticides. It also uses growth hormones in its beef which are restricted in Europe due to links to cancer. US farmers have tried to have these restrictions lifted repeatedly in the past through the World Trade Organisation and it is likely that they will use TTIP to do so again.

The same goes for the environment, where the EU's REACH regulations are far tougher on potentially toxic substances. In Europe a company has to prove a substance is safe before it can be used; in the US the opposite is true: any substance can be used until it is proven unsafe. As an example, the EU currently bans 1,200 substances from use in cosmetics; the US just 12.

3 Banking regulations

TTIP cuts both ways. The UK, under the influence of the all-powerful City of London, is thought to be seeking a loosening of US banking regulations. America's financial rules are tougher than ours. They were put into place after the financial crisis to directly curb the powers of bankers and avoid a similar crisis happening again. TTIP, it is feared, will remove those restrictions, effectively handing all those powers back to the bankers.

4 Privacy

Remember ACTA (the Anti-Counterfeiting Trade Agreement)? It was thrown out by a massive majority in the European Parliament in 2012 after a huge public backlash against what was rightly seen as an attack on individual privacy where internet service providers would be required to monitor people's online activity. Well, it's feared that TTIP could be bringing back ACTA's central elements, proving that if the democratic approach doesn't work, there's always the back door. An easing of data privacy laws and a restriction of public access to pharmaceutical companies' clinical trials are also thought to be on the cards.

5 Jobs

The EU has admitted that TTIP will probably cause unemployment as jobs switch to the US, where labour standards and trade union rights are lower. It has even advised EU members to draw on European support funds to compensate for the expected unemployment. Examples from other similar bi-lateral trade agreements around the world support the case for job losses. The North American Free Trade Agreement (NAFTA) between the US, Canada and Mexico caused the loss of one million US jobs over 12 years, instead of the hundreds of thousands of extra that were promised.

6 Democracy

TTIP's biggest threat to society is its inherent assault on democracy. One of the main aims of TTIP is the introduction of Investor-State Dispute Settlements (ISDS), which allow companies to sue governments if those governments' policies cause a loss of profits. In effect it means unelected transnational corporations can dictate the policies of democratically elected governments.

ISDSs are already in place in other bi-lateral trade agreements around the world and have led to such injustices as in Germany where Swedish energy company Vattenfall is suing the German government for billions of dollars over its decision to phase out nuclear power plants in the wake of the Fukushima disaster in Japan. Here we see a public health policy put into place by a democratically elected government being threatened by an energy giant because of a potential loss of profit. Nothing could be more cynically anti-democratic.

There are around 500 similar cases of businesses versus nations going on around the world at the moment and they are all taking place before 'arbitration tribunals' made up of corporate lawyers appointed on an ad hoc basis, which according to War on Want's John Hilary, are "little more than kangaroo courts" with "a vested interest in ruling in favour of business."

So I don't know about you, but I'm scared. I would vote against TTIP, except... hang on a minute... I can't. Like you, I have no say whatsoever in whether TTIP goes through or not. All I can do is tell as many people about it as possible, as I hope, will you. We may be forced to accept an attack on democracy but we can at least fight against the conspiracy of silence".

An edited version of 'Have you heard about TTIP?' From Lee Williams of the Independent 6 October 2015

http://www.independent.co.uk/voices/comment/what-is-ttip-and-six-reasons-why-the-answer-should-scare-you-9779688.html

Pitched against a fortress of political, corporate and bureaucratic power, the campaign to halt this agreement looked hopeless. But in a miracle of sanity the agreement to totally hand over our sovereignty to US business was halted by the actions of individuals and groups protesting and has since been withdrawn – but the plan starkly demonstrates what Big Corporate is after, and they will keep coming. New secret trade deals between Theresa May and Donald Trump are already underway.

CETA

No sooner than TTIP was stopped, came Ceta, the Comprehensive Economic and Trade Agreement'. From George Monbiot; "This 'trade agreement' threatens to lock in privatisation, making renationalisation (of Britain's railways, say) or attempts by cities to take control of failing public services (as Joseph Chamberlain did in Birmingham in the 19th century, laying the foundations for modern social provision) impossible. Like TTIP, it uses a broad definition of both investment and expropriation to allow corporations to sue governments when they believe their "future anticipated profits" might be threatened by new laws.

Like TTIP, it restricts the ways in which governments may protect their people. It appears to prohibit, for example, rules that would prevent banks from becoming too big to fail. It seems to threaten our planning laws and other commonsense protections.

Anything not specifically exempted from the agreement is considered covered. In other words, if governments do not spot a potential hazard before the hazard emerges, they are stuck with it. The EU appears to have relinquished its ability, for example, to insist that investment and retail banking be separated.

CETA claims to be a trade treaty, but many of its provisions have little to do with trade. They are attempts to circumscribe democracy on behalf of corporate power. Millions of people in Europe and Canada want to emerge from the neoliberal era. But such treaties would lock us into it, allowing the politics we have rejected to govern us beyond the grave.

If parliaments reject this treaty, another deal is being prepared: the Trade in Services Agreement, which the EU is simultaneously negotiating with the US and 21 other nations. Theresa May's government has expressed enthusiasm: her Department for International Trade says: "The UK remains committed to an ambitious Trade in Services Agreement." So much for taking back control.

Corporate lobbyists and their captive governments have been seeking to impose such treaties for more than 20 years, starting with the Multilateral Agreement on Investment (it was destroyed, like TTIP, by massive public protests, in 1998). Working in secrecy, without democratic consent, they will keep returning to the theme, in the hope of wearing down our resistance.

When you are told that the price of liberty is eternal vigilance, this is what it means. This struggle will continue throughout your life. We have to succeed every time; they have to succeed only once. Never drop your guard. Never let them win".

From 'The Transatlantic Trade Deal TTIP May Be Dead, But Something Even Worse Is Coming'. George Monbiot.

https://www.theguardian.com/commentisfree/2016/sep/06/transatla ntic-trade-partnership-ttip-canada-eu

Investigatory Powers Act

From Ewen MacAskill; "A bill giving the UK intelligence agencies and police the most sweeping surveillance powers in the western world has passed into law with barely a whimper, meeting only token resistance over the past 12 months from inside parliament and barely any from outside.

The Investigatory Powers Act...legalises a whole range of tools for snooping and hacking by the security services unmatched by any other country in western Europe or even the US.

The security agencies and police began the year braced for at least some opposition, rehearsing arguments for the debate. In the end, faced with public apathy and an opposition in disarray, the government did not have to make a single substantial concession to the privacy lobby.

US whistleblower Edward Snowden tweeted: *"The UK has just legalised the most extreme surveillance in the history of Western democracy. It goes further than many autocracies."*

Snowden in 2013 revealed the scale of mass surveillance – or bulk data collection as the security agencies prefer to describe it – by the US National Security Agency and the UK's GCHQ, which work in tandem.

But, against a backdrop of fears of Islamist attacks, the privacy lobby has failed to make much headway. Even in Germany, with East Germany's history of mass surveillance by the Stasi and where

Snowden's revelations produced the most outcry, the Bundestag recently passed legislation giving the intelligence agencies more surveillance powers.

The US passed a modest bill last year curtailing bulk phone data collection but the victory of Donald Trump in the US presidential election is potentially a major reverse for privacy advocates. On the campaign trail, Trump made comments that implied he would like to use the powers of the surveillance agencies against political opponents.

The Liberal Democrat peer Lord Strasburger, one of the leading voices against the investigatory powers bill, said:

"We do have to worry about a UK Donald Trump. If we do end up with one, and that is not impossible, we have created the tools for repression. If Labour had backed us up, we could have made the bill better. We have ended up with a bad bill because they were all over the place...The real Donald Trump has access to all the data that the British spooks are gathering and we should be worried about that."

The Investigatory Powers Act legalises powers that the security agencies and police had been using for years without making this clear to either the public or parliament. In October, the investigatory powers tribunal, the only court that hears complaints against MI6, MI5 and GCHQ, ruled that they had been unlawfully collecting massive volumes of confidential personal data without proper oversight for 17 years.

Privacy groups are challenging the surveillance powers in the European court of human rights and elsewhere. Jim Killock, the executive director of Open Rights Group, said:

"The UK now has a surveillance law that is more suited to a dictatorship than a democracy. The state has unprecedented powers to monitor and analyse UK citizens' communications regardless of whether we are suspected of any criminal activity."

Ewen MacAskill. 'Extreme surveillance' becomes UK law with barely a whimper.

https://www.theguardian.com/world/2016/nov/19/extreme-surveillance-becomes-uk-law-with-barely-a-whimper

For a full breakdown of agencies that can now ask for UK citizens' internet browsing history – please see Appendix 1.

The Ministry of Truth

From Tyler Durden; "The US media has indoctrinated the public to assume that any information which is not in compliance with the official government narrative, or dares to criticize the establishment, is also 'fake news'. Thus, it falls under the 'Russian propaganda' umbrella, the scene is now set for the US government to legally crack down on every media outlet that the government deems to be foreign propaganda.

As with any legislation attempting to dodge the public spotlight the Countering Foreign Propaganda and Disinformation Act of 2016 marks a further curtailment of press freedom and another avenue to stultify avenues of accurate information. Introduced by Congressmen Adam Kinzinger and Ted Lieu, H.R. 5181 seeks a "whole-government approach without the bureaucratic restrictions" to counter "foreign disinformation and manipulation," which they believe threaten the world's "security and stability."

In a statement, Obama said that:

"Today, I have signed into law S. 2943, the "National Defense Authorization Act for Fiscal Year 2017." This Act authorizes fiscal year 2017 appropriations principally for the Department of Defense and for Department of Energy national security programs, provides vital benefits for military personnel and their families, and includes authorities to facilitate ongoing operations around the globe. It continues many critical authorizations necessary to ensure that we are able to sustain our momentum in countering the threat posed by the Islamic State of Iraq and the Levant and to reassure our European allies, as well as many new authorizations that, among other things, provide the Departments of Defense and Energy more flexibility in countering cyber-attacks and our adversaries' use of unmanned aerial vehicles."

Obama Quietly Signs The 'Countering Disinformation And Propaganda Act' Into Law by Tyler Durden

Just like that, the US Ministry of Truth is officially born. Already the Whitehouse is excluding certain news producers from briefings because they don't like the narratives.

Croneyism

From Jon Stone; "The Conservatives have been accused of an attempt to hide party cronyism after quietly switching the way that the political affiliations of people given top public-sector roles are recorded.

Critics claimed the switch in the way affiliations are recorded will mean Tories could 'hand top jobs to their mates', just months after officials blocked part of Mr Cameron's resignation honours list in which aides and friends were handed baubles including a peerage and knighthoods.

It comes just 24 hours after Theresa May's administration was accused of making a separate change to how public appointments are approved that would make it easier for ministers in the future to pick political allies for senior jobs.

But it is the 'methodology change' in how political affiliations are recorded that will mask any glut of appointments in the final year of Mr Cameron's administration.

The co-leader of the Green party, Jonathan Bartley, told The Independent:

"It's no wonder more and more people are disillusioned with politics when we have a system that doesn't just fail to stop politicians handing top jobs to their mates, but also deliberately seeks to hide what's going on.

"We've long called for transparency to be the watchword when it comes to political appointments and the revolving doors that exist between industry and government. Sadly though, cronyism is still the order of the day."

Labour shadow minister Andrew Gwynne branded the change a 'gross distortion of government data'. He told The Independent:

"These changes attempt to hide the true scale of the Tories' power grab on our democracy – hiding the extent to which Tory allies have been snuck into the boardrooms of public institutions...It's a gross distortion of government data, flies in the face of transparency and must be stopped."

Mr Cameron was dragged into a cronyism row this summer after an independent scrutiny committee blocked part of his resignation honours list, refusing to support an award to a City businessman who raised an estimated £70m for the party.

Theresa May refused to intervene to block the list, which Labour's deputy leader Tom Watson branded an "old boy's network" and Liberal Democrat leader Tim Farron said "would embarrass a medieval court".

Edited version of 'Tories 'masking true scale' of political cronyism with quiet rule change. Jon Stone Political Correspondent for the Independent

http://www.independent.co.uk/news/uk/politics/honours-cronies-david-cameron-tories-a7492906.html

Taxation and Slavery

Our political systems have come to tax us for a percentage of the energy we spend in work-to-earn-money. The more successful we are in earning money, the more energy the government of the day can take. Added to this system are local taxes, invisible taxes, stealth taxes, property taxes, inheritance taxes, value added taxes and so on. If we are employed, more and more of our energy goes into feeding this system which is essentially flawed and responsible for the continued devastation of our planet through pollution – a side effect of this essentially flawed economy. If you don't want to invest your earnings or pension in weapons, bombs, slavery and pharmacueticals – it's actually quite hard to avoid doing so.

Have you considered in terms of a percentage how much the system itself takes from you? Not only everything we earn but everything we buy, our travel costs, food, clothes, homes, lives – all taxed. 50% would be a conservative guestimate probably more like 60% or 80%. That's more than half the time at least that we spend in employment to feed a system we don't like with our energy. No wonder people get ill.

The more our energy is involved with the economy, the more our energy is taxed – taking money for a whole host of things we may not approve. In the world of work we are tied into a system that takes our energy and does things that we don't like with it. Our success in life is often defined as how well we prosper within this system. And to do that there are certain questions we have to stop asking, such as 'Where is all this energy going' or 'What's it actually doing' – 'What's the point'?

"You know in the West we have built a large, beautiful ship. It has all the comforts in it. But one thing is missing: It has no compass and does not know where to go."

Albert Einstein

We have a political and economic system that is decreasing personal liberty, lining its own pockets whilst bringing in new 'austerity measures' for the rest of us, increasing beaurocracy and taxation and overseeing the systematic destruction of the environment through industrialisation. It seems to spend most of the time just making up more stupid laws that have not been properly thought through and are just short-term, knee jerk reactions to fundamental changes in reality. Force all the unemployed into jobs? What jobs?

What if the system itself is the problem? It seems totally screwed up and we seem presently on a conveyor belt to planetary self-destruction. What if you want to get off?

This is very difficult because we are all investors by default in this system, even just by having a bank account we are damned, tainted by Mammon. In order to feed ourselves physically we have invented money that is held in banks. As soon as we enter this system of promisary notes and hold bank accounts we are investors by default in slavery, child prostitution, armaments, pharmaceutical industries, deforestation, criminality, and so on – everything that money does. If you pay into a pension to secure your old-age then once again you are often tied to investment in undesirable outcomes, the bombs dropped on Syria, the pollution of dirty energy, the human misery of sex slaves or drug addicts – everything that money does.

There are many hypocrisies in being a person with spiritual intent, manifesting at a physical level. I am interested in consciousness shifting / raising, finding an exciting paradigm of energy awareness and holistic health and happiness in my life. I see myself as primarily a spiritual being, manifesting at a physical level, rather than the other way round. I feel that 'the system' has always made this life choice as hard as can be. The system itself is a parasite on the human spirit.

The answer for me was quite straightforward. Take my energy out of 'the system' and invest it in things that work. Become energy independent, grow and make rather than buy food and consumables. Invest time in local economies of exchange and barter. Need less, want less, – reduce, recycle, re-use, repair. Simpling down is a great way to go and definitely improves the enjoyment of life that money, increasingly, can so rarely buy. In the balance between 'standard of living' and 'quality of life' – my disinvolvement with the system gives me a good quality of life.

It worries me how few people seem to question that it seems normal to get dressed for work in the mornings and drive through polluting traffic to work at a job you don't really like to pay for the car and the clothes and the house you leave empty all day so you can afford to live in it.

The Government are very careful about who they target for the next stealth tax to hold up the Treasury. Rather than applying blanket taxes on us all, like the Poll Tax (now Council Tax) which created massive resistance, they target minority groups, outside the norm, with no internal cohesion – taking legal rights from absent fathers, benefits from single mothers, pensions from pensioners, human rights from travellers, taxing the poor with extra bedrooms and so on. Easy targets who are unlikely to collectively rebel due to no group identity or cohesion. Often they will work hand-in-hand with mass media to demonise a group before applying stealth taxation.

So if you are working all the hours you have to pay childcare costs, or if you are in energy poverty because it is so expensive to buy fuel, of you can't afford to buy food or are forced to have a lodger – look around for people in the same situation – there are mutual solutions to these problems that take you outside of reliance on a system that is essentially broken beyond repair.

The Myth of Sustainability

In ecological / economic terms 'sustainability' (as used in the 1987 Brundtland Report) meant *'development that meets the needs of the present without compromising the ability of future generations to meet their own needs'*. Another definition is: *'improving the quality of human life while living quietly within the carrying capacity of supporting eco-systems'*. Unfortunately this has turned out to be 'greenwash'. The values of industrialism it seems are not compatible with those of life itself.

The use of the term sustainability in this context today is often corrupted, even by supposedly mainstream politicians, to 'something we can keep going' in general business term, hence hiding the developed meaning. This process of popularisation / corruption of word meanings (aka dumbing down) is one reason why we need to redefine concepts and reach for new meanings and ideas in new words. What has become clear is that 'sustaining' an economy of 'business as usual' is not compatible with keeping the nature on our planet.

The idea of sustainability begs the question 'What it is that we are actually trying to sustain?'

- an outdated cultural narrative?

- an unhealthy conception of the relationship between humanity and nature?

- business as usual in a deeply inequitable world?

- a structurally dysfunctional system and worldview?

We need to search for new ways to restore ecosystems, celebrate cultural diversity, initiate a worldview change, and facilitate the transition towards diverse cultures that regenerate not just vital resources and community resilience, but contribute to the health and vitality of nature's life support systems. Such cultures will assure the future of life as a whole and not merely sustain a humanity divorced from its roots and alienated from the ground of its own being.

Free Market Economy

"The Global 'free market economy' is inherently an enemy to the natural world, to human health and freedom, to industrial workers, and to farmers and others in land-use economies; and furthermore, that it is inherently an enemy to good work and good economic practice."

Wendell Berry

"From top to bottom, first is the rise of what we now call capitalism itself, specifically how the presence of social dominance has become obscured by 'free trade.' All major historical economic systems since the Neolithic Revolution have been market-based in the sense that the root socioeconomic orientation of competition, exploitation, and scarcity has been dominant.

The molding of modern-day capitalism over time was inevitable as more complex labour roles and technology advanced. In this, the once-obvious social inequities and undemocratic power imbalance of early societies slowly became cloaked by the idealism of 'free market democracy'. Unlike in earlier eras, which featured intolerant government monarchs, abject slavery, and other more primitive forms of dictatorial power and direct oppression, this new structure provided the needed illusion of democratic participation, rights, and freedom by structurally submerging social dominance within the mass competitive act of 'free trade.'

The beauty of this means of social dominance is that it facilitates the pretense that totalitarianism doesn't exist. Kings and regimes no longer wield total control over the lives of their subjects. Rather, power and wealth remain concentrated by way of the incentive for competitive advantage in the market - a business structure that is provably undemocratic and rigged to favor a small, transient minority in the same basic manner (yet obscured) by which a monarch once exerted control."

The New Human Rights Movement, Peter Joseph

"Make no mistake. The greatest destroyer of ecology. The greatest source of waste, depletion and pollution. The greatest purveyor of violence, war, crime, poverty, animal abuse and inhumanity. The greatest generator of personal and social neurosis, mental disorders, depression, anxiety. Not to mention the greatest source of social paralysis, stopping us from moving into new methodologies for personal health, global sustainability and progress on this planet, is not some corrupt government or legislation. Not some rogue corporation or banking cartel. Not some flaw of human nature and not some secret cabal that controls the world. It is the socioeconomic system itself at its very foundation."

Peter Joseph, founder of The Zeitgeist Movement.

I could go on ad-infinitum providing examples of how our socioeconomic system of capitalism has not only failed – but has brought us all to the brink of disaster, but I want to concentrate on solutions. But first, let us look at the control systems that allow for this ridiculous state of affairs.

3. THE CONTROL SYSTEMS

"As long as the general population is passive, apathetic, diverted to consumerism or hatred of the vulnerable then the powerful can do as they please and those who survive will be left to contemplate the outcome."

Noam Chomsky

Energy

It is not only *'corporately controlled mass media hegemony'* that acts as a control system for our thoughts. The 'wetiko' philosophy is embedded into all of our systems, not just media.

Our news on energy for the UK is full of austerity measures for energy, for example Emily Gosden, Energy Editor for the Telegraph reports:

"Britain will be forced to rely on imports and costly emergency measures to prevent blackouts, official data suggests. Britain's energy supply forecasts have plunged 'into the red' next winter for the first time on record, suggesting the country will be forced to rely on imports and costly emergency interventions to prevent blackouts.

Figures from National Grid show that on current plans there will not be enough power plants operating in the UK market to keep the lights on for most of December, January and February [2018].

The supply gap has emerged because a series of old, polluting power stations have been shut down, while hardly any replacement plants are being built."

http://www.telegraph.co.uk/news/earth/energy/12175367/UK-energy-supply-forecasts-into-the-red-for-first-time-next-winter.html

Ignoring the article bias against renewables (eg energy does not just come from power stations), it presents energy as an asset we do not have enough of, a scarce asset. In whose interest is promoting energy as a scarce and limited asset?

In full sun, you can safely assume about 100 watts of solar energy per square foot. If you assume 12 hours of sun per day, this equates to 438,000 watt-hours per square foot per year. Based on 27,878,400 square feet per square mile, sunlight bestows a whopping 12.2 trillion watt-hours per square mile per year.

With these assumptions, figuring out how much solar energy hits the entire planet is relatively simple. 12.2 trillion watt-hours converts to 12,211 gigawatt-hours, and based on 8,760 hours per year, and 197 million square miles of earth's surface (including the oceans), the earth receives about 274 million gigawatt-years of solar energy, which translates to an astonishing 8.2 million 'quads' of Btu energy per year. A 'quad Btu' refers to one quadrillion British Thermal Units of energy, a common term used by energy economists. The entire human race currently uses about 400 quads of energy (in all forms) per year. Put another way, just the solar energy hitting the earth exceeds the total energy consumed by humanity by a factor of over 20,000 times. And that is just the sun's energy.

Yet the takeup of renewables is constantly set back because of the vested interest of companies in the fossil fuel business, (who now 'own' our governments) resulting in confrontations over oil pipelines, fracking and all the other grisly business. We are fed the lie over and over again, energy is scarce, energy is limited when in fact the *whole universe is made of energy.* So – if we live in a universe made of energy – why are we supposedly 'running out'?

We are rather young as a species. Our non-renewable sources of energy such as oil, coal, natural gas and nuclear power are becoming scarce (or too dirty and dangerous) just at the moment we have realised that everything is made of energy. We have been so stuck in a world of non-renewables that the groundwork on harvesting the infinite energy of the universe is still being done. Information concerning this is often repressed in the interest of global multinationals who want our money and sponsor our governments.

Imagine – making us go out to work in jobs all day to pay for energy which is actually FREE and INFINITE and EVERYWHERE. What a shocker if people found out how to harvest their own!

There are many sources of renewable energy: wind, water, geothermal, solar, tidal, biomass, even natural electricity and hydrogen (secondary energy sources) – methods of harvesting them are getting easier – some people are even making 'harvesting devices' for energy out of rubbish!

You might think that with all this energy falling from the sun, tidal power, wind power and other renewable sources that the solution to our energy problems would be easy – simply switch over. The problem is that vested interest has kept the development of alternatives 'quiet' over the last 25 years or so. The Tory trend in the UK is presently about disinvestment in alternative power and in the US Government Big Oil is King. Yee Hah!

Our planet is rich in energy. Enough energy simply falls on the planet from the sun in 40 minutes to supply all of our needs for a year. We are running out of several forms of fossil energy at present, hence the discussions of 'peak oil' and the like. Energy produced from oil, gas, coal and other natural resources has reached its 'peak' – supplies are dwindling while our need for energy is increasing to work our homes, our transport and our industries. Multinationals with vested interests would sooner grasp at straws like 'fracking' than change their dirty ways. Despite the ongoing global tragedy at Fukushima, others want to invest in nuclear power (at cost to the taxpayer) in order to keep power generation centralised and monopolised, eg keep the power structures the same. Given that our environment is suffering from all this extraction and the resultant pollution, its better to leave it in the ground.

The decentralisation of energy supply is a huge issue in the economies of energy. The power that pays for governments often comes from large industry and centralised monopolies are a large part of the capitalism that runs our economy. Harvesting our own energy supplies 'from the wild' still runs counter to the interests of a culture based on 'consuming' what is supplied to them from a centralised controller, in order to create money streams. This is why the issues of microgeneration or even of 'using less energy' are barely discussed at government level – they run contrary to the ideology of consumerism and a growth economy. Presently new legislation is being contrived in the UK to tax people who have invested in the self-generation of energy.

Media

"The masses have never thirsted after truth. Whoever can supply them with illusions is easily their master; whoever attempts to destroy their illusions is always their victim."

Gustave Le Bon

"It's much easier to fool people than to convince them that they have been fooled — such is the nature of confirmation bias and other psychological tools of manipulation. Breaking free of the ancient, historical 'constant' of mind control is an ongoing process of waking up out of a state of denial. Spiritual emergence and awakening involves a physiological break from the consensus social agreements of our planetary cultures."

Karlos Kukuburra

Figure 2: Simple but wrong or complex but right both lead to the edge

Once you start to see the normative control systems built into our television programmes and adverts it is hard not to see them as a form of abuse. They are relentless and utterly entrenched into every TV drama, movie, quiz show, story and news programme.

It is said that if you don't follow the news you are uninformed as to what is going on in the world. But if you do follow the news you are most likely misinformed because the presentation of the news is selected according to an agenda and presented with a political bias.

Whether we are watching Russell Brand's 'Trews', reading the Daily Mail or Express, listening to the World Service on the BBC or a commercial radio station in the US – each media stream has a slightly different emphasis and audience as to what is important in the world. To create interest the choice of news stories revolve mainly around qualities of drama, conflict and scenes of visual impact. All of them support the status quo. OK not Russell Brand!

There may seem to be a lot of choice in media streams. But increasingly media sources are owned by fewer and fewer hands - standardising the news which is often contracted second-hand from news agencies anyway. In the US for example there are about 1500 newspapers, 1100 magazines, 9000 radio stations, 1500 TV stations and 2400 publishers. Lots of choice you might think. They are all owned by just three corporations – lots of choice, but no options!

These different streams mostly promote the 'status quo', the normative values of our society. For example, most news will often include a report on 'the economy'. Constant announcements that the economy has 'grown' (or not) on media seem so central to our way of life that we consider that this is normal, important, desirable even. This is part of the constant conditioning supplied by media.

'News values' make up the criteria that decides the 'news' we see in mainstream media. This combines with the editorial bias of the owner or editor of that media stream, and its potential for revealing advertising revenue from the audience it seeks. It is very much a part of our Western way. Our cultural norms have dictated the view of the world we expect and this is reflected in the values of the mainstream news source we choose as most believable.

News Values

Media theorists such as Galtang and Ruge give insights into the values that dictate the 'newsworthiness' of our mainstream media news:

Frequency: Events that occur suddenly and fit well with the news organization's schedule are more likely to be reported than those that occur gradually or at inconvenient times of day or night. Long-term trends are not likely to receive much coverage. **Negativity**: Bad news is more newsworthy than good news.

Unexpectedness: If an event is out of the ordinary it will have a greater effect than something that is an everyday occurrence.

Unambiguity: Events whose implications are clear make for better copy than those that are open to more than one interpretation, or where any understanding of the implications depends on first understanding the complex background in which the events take place.

Personalization: Events that can be portrayed as the actions of individuals will be more attractive than one in which there is no such "human interest."

Meaningfulness: This relates to the sense of identification the audience has with the topic. "Cultural proximity" is a factor here — stories concerned with people who speak the same language, look the same, and share the preoccupations as the audience receive more coverage than those concerned with people who speak different languages, look different and have different preoccupations.

Reference to elite nations: Stories concerned with global powers receive more attention than those concerned with less influential nations.

Reference to elite persons: Stories concerned with celebrity, the rich, powerful, famous and infamous get more coverage.

Conflict: Opposition of people or forces resulting in a dramatic effect. Stories with conflict are always quite newsworthy.

Consonance: Stories that fit with the media's expectations receive more coverage than those that defy them (and for which they are thus unprepared). Note this appears to conflict with unexpectedness above. However, consonance really refers to the media's readiness to report an item.

Continuity: A story that is already in the news gathers a kind of inertia. This is partly because the media organizations are already in place to report the story, and partly because previous reportage may have made the story more accessible to the public (making it less ambiguous).

Composition: Stories must compete with one another for space in the media. For instance, editors may seek to provide a balance of different types of coverage, so that if there is an excess of foreign news for instance, the least important foreign story may have to make way for an item concerned with the domestic news. In this way the prominence given to a story depends not only on its own news values but also on those of competing stories. (Galtung and Ruge, 1965)

Competition: Commercial or professional competition between media may lead journalists to endorse the news value given to a story by a rival.

Co-optation: A story that is only marginally newsworthy in its own right may be covered if it is related to a major running story.

Prefabrication: A story that is marginal in news terms but written and available may be selected ahead of a much more newsworthy story that must be researched and written from the ground up.

Predictability: An event is more likely to be covered if it has been pre-scheduled. (Bell, 1991)

Time constraints: Traditional news media such as radio, television and daily newspapers have strict deadlines and a short production cycle, which selects for items that can be researched and covered quickly.

Logistics: Although eased by the availability of global communications even from remote regions, the ability to deploy and control production and reporting staff, and functionality of technical resources can determine whether a story is covered. (Schlesinger, 1987)

From Wikipedia: http://en.wikipedia.org/wiki/News_values

These selection values mean that the news we see is very specifically selected to control our expectations of the world. We choose to be fed a media stream that most endorses our view of the world. Using these values it is easy to see why stories such as 'Global Warming', 'Melting Icecaps', a 'quiet and gradual revolution of attitude', or the 'daily radioactive waste pouring from Fukushima into the oceans' doesn't fit into news. Because they are ongoing, they emerge slowly over a long period of time, they don't really become news until they cause storm winds that rip the roof off a celebrity's house, floods that sink a town or the finding of a two-headed salmon.

Our biased positions were deliciously satirised by Bernard Woolley in a 1987 version of the TV show '*Yes Prime minister!*

"The Daily Mirror is read by people who think they run the country;

The Guardian is read by people who think they ought to run the country;

The Times is read by people who actually do run the country;

The Daily Mail is read by the wives of the people who run the country;

The Financial Times is read by people who own the country;

The Morning Star is read by people who think the country ought to be run by another country;

And the Daily Telegraph is read by people who think it already is."

Sir Humphrey: *"Prime Minister, what about the people who read the Sun?"*

Bernard Woolley: *"Sun readers don't care who runs the country, as long as she's got big tits".*

"We accept the status quo of warfare, fear, environmental destruction, greed, corruption, poisoned health and false scarcity because we've been herded into traps which hold us hostage with false beliefs and the appearance of comfort. In reality, though, breaking through these traps would allow us to apply the principles of peace, sustainability, exploration, acceptance and progress to improving the human condition."

Sigmund Fraud

Online News

As postmodernism and new technology collide, our news sources online are becoming more fragmented and we are often free to choose not just the 'values' we prefer but also the news streams focused in specific interest zones. The internet, (at least until it becomes totally controlled) has bought us some alternative options and ways of gathering our news. Back to the 'filter bubbles' concept.

For example right now my Google News settings might bring me news streams showing reports on British Government Solar PV Tarrif and news on Codex Alimentarius, Monsanto and international trade agreements. I am more likely to read a blog than a newspaper and generally pick up news of World import from BBC World Radio. My Facebook friends all publish positive and visionary articles otherwise I unfriend them, because I want thoughts and links that help me believe I live in the world I want to! Yes – I'm a hypocrite too!

The democratisation of knowledge on the internet is certainly part of an ongoing evolution of consciousness in humans. Wikipedia, criticised early-on for inaccuracies is a growing resource of people friendly information. When I think of the amount of information at my fingertips now compared with twenty or thirty years ago, the changes are just immense. Social media too, allows people more ready access to peer group discussion and helps them to form values that, (if they can get their faces out of their phones) can lead to productive activism.

It seems to me that part of the transition process from the 'industrial growth society' we have now to a 'life-sustaining civilisation' depends on us changing our 'stories' and part of this is certainly entrenched in news values. News from the 'industrial growth society' tells us stories of austerity, gloom, doom and despondency, how bad it all is, because these negative beliefs serve capitalism. Pessimism preserves the status quo. Think for example the psychological effect of articles like the following:

Telegraph: Doomsday clock for global market crash strikes one minute to midnight as central banks lose control.

China currency devaluation signals endgame leaving equity markets free to collapse under the weight of impossible expectations. When the banking crisis crippled global markets seven years ago, central bankers stepped in as lenders of last resort. Profligate private-sector loans were moved on to the public-sector balance sheet and vast money-printing gave the global economy room to heal.

Time (Xetra: 17T.DE – news) is now rapidly running out. From China to Brazil, the central banks have lost control and at the same time the global economy is grinding to a halt. It (Other OTC: ITGL – news) is only a matter of time before stock markets collapse under the weight of their lofty expectations and record valuations...

Yahoo News: Earth Is Now 'In The Red' – We Used Up This Year's Resources Yesterday.

Every year, 'Overshoot Day' comes earlier and earlier. Human beings have just exhausted the planet's supply of natural resources – meaning we are 'in the red' from now on.

Every year, 'Overshoot Day' – the point where we go into ecological 'debt', in terms of the amount of carbon we emit, and crops we use up – comes earlier. This year, it arrived yesterday [16.08.15] – six years earlier than it did in 2014, according to an estimate by the Global Footprint Network.

The GFN says that our consumption began to exceed the planet's capacity by the early 1970s – and as the world's population expands, it has been getting worse each year.

Humanity's carbon footprint alone more than doubled since the early 1970s, when the world went into ecological overshoot.

Yahoo News: Human Beings 'Could Die Out' In New Mass Extinction.

Many scientists believe the next mass extinction event is already underway. Human beings could be wiped out in the next mass extinction on Earth – and our huge numbers won't save us, scientists believe. Many believe that we are on the brink of a sixth 'mass extinction' event – caused not by an asteroid, but by human beings.

Researchers from the University of Leeds analysed fossils from the Jurassic and Triassic periods to see how species were affected by a mass extinction event. Around 200 million years ago, around 80% of species were wiped out by an event thought to have been triggered by volcanic eruptions and climate change.

Through the media we see a world of fear and intimidation, simplifying complex stories into black and white, us and them, creating personal and nationalistic divides to prevent any meaningful response. We are fed distractions in terms of 'celebrity' and stories of the meritocracy like Strictly or X factor. They show shiny bling, meaningless gossip, endless choice with no real options. Using the power of media, the stories, the news, we are fed messages of *fear and intimidation*. We are offered *distractions* and *easy answers* where it is either option A or Option B, because this divides us into two opposing camps to keep us distracted and ineffective.

Below is an example of what the media might be telling us, compared to what they do actually tell us.

What you need to know about:	The news we get in mainstream media:
Why bats are dying by the millions	Who got murdered
Why bees are dying by the billions	Lyndsay Lohan
Why birds populations are plunging	Who said what that doesn't matter
Ocean acidification	Kanye West and Kim Kardashian
The melting ice caps	Car chases
Deforestation	Justin Beiber
Dangers of natural gas fracking	Who is getting divorced
Tar sands pollution and its dangers	The First Lady's workout routine
The toxic radioactive waste streaming out of Fukushima into the Pacific	Sex scandals
GMOs, Monsanto and the problems caused by toxic farming policies	The stock report
Potential food shortages because of drought, soil depletion and the plunge in wildlife populations	Who is gay
Polluted and depleted aquifers	How many cars are selling
How to grow food	Who got arrested
Hazards of industrial pollution	Drama in D.C
Lies your government is feeding you	The housing market
Lies the financial system is spewing	Sports drama
Lies about the tax system	Misinformation about history

How your rights are being violated	Who got an award
Damaged, clunky, aging nuclear power plants and their dangers	Courtroom scandals
The realities of war	Gas prices
Depleted uranium bomb residue from the ongoing wars and how it is spreading via weather patterns	'Reality' show drama
Growth of the prison industry	What's being built
Lies about the War on Drugs	Whatever subtly perpetuates fear
How to disconnect from fossil fuels	Travel and leisure stuff
Permaculture and sustainable living	Who bought something expensive
Importance of organic foods	What haircut to get
How to work with your neighbours	A little about racism and sexism
How to become more self-sufficient	Corporate products to buy
How to improve your community	Who had a baby
Air pollution where you live	What Trump did next
How to get pure water	What colour to wear

"The smart way to keep people passive and obedient is to strictly limit the spectrum of acceptable opinion but to allow lively debate within that spectrum."

Noam Chomsky

Money

"This is the greatest trap of all, enslaving nearly everyone on our planet. At the root of this deception is the general belief in money, that is, in the belief that money has more value than life itself and is therefore more precious than anything life has to offer. Because of this, countless schemes, scams, fiat systems, debt-enslavement programs, frauds, and thefts are able to syphon the energy and time of human beings, leading us nowhere but to our own ruin.

The monetary system we have today operates in this way, with a tiny ruling elite having devised and now controlling an international system of manipulation which gives unlimited power to those who create money without having to produce anything of actual value."

Sigmund Fraud

Since the beginning of the Industrial Revolution consumer capitalism has journeyed on a path of stupidity and futility, based on the belief that we can forever use our capital assets, the earth itself, as a form of income.

We are presently using up the resources of this planet as if we had three planets to spend. It is clear too that government, utterly resistant to change, will be the last to admit to this, as their entire reason for existence is built around servicing 'the economy', the monstrous lie, the massive elephant in the room that we ignore at our peril.

So we have stories about money. The banks at the centre of this stupidity are slowly going bust due to such things as 'Fractional Reserve Banking' – a story they have for lending money that they don't have. Added to this criminal scam is counterfeiting, the artificial printing of money which isn't there because it has no associated value. This is supported, even encouraged by government and explained as 'quantitative easing'. Just print some more...

"The modern banking system manufactures money out of nothing. The process is perhaps the most outstanding piece of sleight of hand that was ever invented."

Former Bank of England Director

Central banks repress interest rates to hide the real cost of money and then blame the retail banks for 'manipulating libor'. The 'deposit guarantees' supported by government legislation mean that when the banks do go bust through their own incompetence and chicanery, the taxpayer picks up the cost. This is direct theft.

As it stands, politicians have managed to protect the banks (apart from in Iceland) while everyone else takes the pain. As the cuts pinch the poor and the rich get no poorer, it will become clear whose interests are being served. As worker militancy grows and protests become more frequent, the demand for ever stronger, authoritative states will become louder, civil liberties will be curtailed (again), and those at the top of the tree will tell us that they have some special right.

"Banking was conceived in iniquity and born in sin. Bankers own the earth. Take it away from them but leave them the power to create money and control credit and with the flick of a pen, they will create enough money to buy it back again. But if you want to continue as the slaves of bankers and pay the cost of your own slavery, let them continue to create money and to control credit."

Sir Joshua Stamp, Director of the Bank of England

Iceland

Over the last 200 years, 83 countries have gone bankrupt. More recently in Europe, Cyprus, Ireland, Portugal, Spain and Greece have all received massive bank bailouts making 'austerity' a household word in these countries. The exception though, is Iceland and for this very reason it is worth taking a closer look at how the crooked banks got their come-uppance. From the BBC; How did Iceland clean up its banks?

"The 2008 global financial crisis hit Iceland hard. The currency crashed, unemployment soared and the stock market was more or less wiped out.

But unlike other Western economies, the Icelandic government let its three major banks fail and went after reckless bankers. Many senior executives have been jailed and the country's ex-prime minister Geir Haarde was also put on trial, becoming the first world leader to face criminal prosecution arising from the turmoil, although he was subsequently cleared of negligence. Experts talked to the BBC World Service Inquiry programme.

Gudrun Johnsen: The reckoning

Gudrun Johnsen was on the special commission set up to learn lessons from Iceland's banking collapse.

"The banks were 10 times the GDP of Iceland; 20 times the state budget. They were too big to bail out...The stock market collapsed: 80% of the stock market was wiped out overnight. Shareholders were badly hurt. About every other business in Iceland became technically bankrupt...97% of the banking sector collapsed in a matter of three days, and I hope I will not witness this anywhere in the world again.

People felt very let down. They were very angry and took to the streets. Two or three per cent of the entire nation gathered in front of parliament demanding answers.

The government demanded that the banks decrease the debt of households [owing more than the value of their house], and that people would not be driven into bankruptcy...The government also set up a special agency where people in big financial trouble could apply for debt forgiveness.

Parliament had to respond to the outcry and set up a Special Investigation Commission, equipped with enormous data privileges so it could reveal the truth behind the collapse...It found the assets of the banks and the loans had been extended into a cobweb: firm A owns firm B, which owns firm C and, sometimes firm C owns firm A. There was virtually very little or no equity in those businesses. The operations are entirely dependent on credit from the banks.

What also came to light was that those who owned these pyramids of corporations were in the ownership of the largest shareholders of the banks themselves. That was very worrisome - we had a financial system that was really opaque. The bankers didn't really know how much equity there was to be matched against the loans they were extending...If you don't know exactly what happened, you don't know what type of behaviour you need to correct, and cultural change is really difficult. There was a benefit in the entire system going down.

We know what failed and as a consequence we were able to clean house pretty quickly."

Olafur Hauksson

Olafur Hauksson was a special prosecutor working on the collapsed bank cases in Iceland. They have brought 28 cases, with more than 60 prosecutions.

"It's been quite time-consuming: in one of the biggest cases we have 22,000 pages...After the three biggest banks failed, the Financial Supervisory Authority took them over and put in Resolution Committees. These were obligated to have auditors go through the books and return a report to the Supervisory Authority. They were obligated to give us information of anything suspicious.

In the beginning, we thought we may find something that was linked to the bank collapse itself; someone trying to take his chances because of the confusion of the crisis. But what came up was that many of the cases that we investigated stretched back several years...It was difficult to decide the difference between criminality and crazy banking, but we were more focused on how they gave their loans out; if they followed proper procedures. If they didn't, that was an indication of some wrongdoing...We had an inside fraud case, and a manager in the Ministry of Finance received two years' imprisonment. Then we had the Exeter Case. The CEO of that bank and the chairman got four and four and a half years' imprisonment...We had an inside fraud case [which got] 12 months' imprisonment; breaches on the Company Act [which got] six and eight months' imprisonment and the lawyer was revoked...Then we had a market manipulation case and fraudulent loans case connecting to Landsbanki. They got three and a half years.

The CEO for all of the Banki (Icelandic banks) received 18 months, and one of the brokers received nine months. Then we have the BK case. Four were found guilty: two received four years, one received three and one received two.

There has been huge conflict in the courtrooms. It has been a big fight. They were testing on each and every inch of our cases...I do not think that we'd be able to establish faith in the system without this being dealt with. It is always about trust."

Asgeir Jonsson

Asgeir Jonsson is the former chief economist at Kaupthing Bank.

"In European banking, there is an unwillingness to accept losses. If you look at how the central banks in the UK and the US and in Europe responded, they printed money...We could not print money, so we had to face the reality. No-one really knows how all the money printing that has been taking place in the major economies of the West will end."

Dr Jay Cullen

Dr Jay Cullen is a lecturer in banking and finance law at the University of Sheffield.

"It's difficult to draw parallels from the Icelandic experience...Iceland experienced a massive increase in the size of its banking system over a very short period of time from about 2000 onwards...I'm not sure that the Icelandic financial system was as important to the performance of the Icelandic economy as say, the City of London is to the UK. The UK economy is much more developed than Iceland's. It's much more reliant upon financial services as a whole.

The frauds involved were overt. There was substantial market manipulation going on, insider trading. These practices did occur in the UK and the US, but they weren't systemic. There was fraud in the US mortgage market, but at fairly low levels. Perhaps the criminal law ought to have bitten, or been employed more vociferously.

The power of the banking lobby in the UK and the US is such that it's politically very difficult to make an enemy of big business...There has to be a fundamental change in the structure of the banking system, and that requires huge political will and sacrifice, and it's not evident to me that exists, because so little has changed since 2008...Now in the US, the banks are even larger than they were pre-2008. They are not only too big to fail, they are too big to manage and possibly too big to exist. The old phrase was, 'Main Street will never again bail out Wall Street.'

That's a noble claim, but the evidence suggests that in the UK and the US, and also in the eurozone, where several countries simply have broken banking systems, the taxpayers are still on the hook. Very little has been done, and the day of reckoning is potentially around the corner."

Medicine

Our whole structure around health and medicine also houses stories.

1. You are not responsible (or knowledgeable enough of) your own body to make it well if it goes wrong.

2. If it goes wrong you take it to a 'qualified' allopathic expert (eg a doctor) who will tell you what to do and will usually prescribe an intervention based on pills and surgery or some other treatment that creates profit for huge international pharmaceutical industries.

Don't get me wrong! Western medicine has, in the past, produced 'world saving' vaccines and antibiotics. It has created drugs and surgical techniques that do utterly amazing things. It has virtually eliminated all the serious communicable diseases (in the First World) such as leprosy, plague, tuberculosis, tetanus, syphilis, rheumatic fever, pneumonia, meningitis, polio, septicaemia. There are very few women dying in childbirth compared to the past.

Western medicine has been, and is, a triumph in the face of these problems which worried us back then the way diabetes, dementia, cancer and heart disease worry us today. Even the big medical problems of the of 1930's and 40's have literally vanished.

But the age of infectious disease has given way to the age of chronic disorders. The major killers today are heart and vascular disease, chronic degenerative diseases and cancer, largely incurable and increasing in incidence. The strategies that worked so well for all but eliminating acute infectious diseases just don't seem to work for chronic and degenerative conditions.

"The prevalence of asthma, multiple sclerosis, chronic fatigue, immune deficiency syndrome, HIV and a host of other debilitating conditions is increasing. Conventional biomedicine - so strikingly successful in the treatment of overwhelming infections, surgical and medical emergencies and congenital defects, has been unable to stem the tide of these conditions".

James Gordon M.D., Washington, D.C.

During the time of Sir Isaac Newton the human body was viewed as an intricate biological machine. The Universe was an orderly, predictable but divine mechanism, a 'grand clockwork'. Although hundreds of years have passed, Western scientific medicine still holds the same basic philosophy, but is more sophisticated in studying biological mechanisms at a molecular level.

The first Newtonian approaches were essentially surgical. The body was seen as if it were a complex plumbing system. If it went wrong the offending piece was removed or bypassed. These days instead of using knives, drugs are often used to do more or less the same things.

Humans though, are far more than walking sacks of chemicals. The animating life-force central to other medical systems is an energy that is not addressed by modern scientific methodology and there are no Western medical models that explain what it is and what it does. It is misguided by the concept that all illnesses are cured by physically repairing or eliminating abnormal cells. This is partly due to a conflict between Western and Eastern philosophies and has its roots in the division of science and religion along with the destruction of folk medicine in both U.S. and Europe.

The strategies that worked so well for tackling acute infectious diseases are inappropriate for dealing with chronic and degenerative conditions. Patients with these can be at best increasingly 'patched up' by orthodox treatments but at spiralling health care costs and this plays directly into the hands of those with vested interests. Medical methodology in a 'quantum' reality is being held back by large corporate interest in league with government legislation. After all when you are diagnosed with cancer you are suddenly worth (a minimum of) $300,000 to the cancer industry.

"As a retired physician, I can honestly say that unless you are in a serious accident, your best chance of living to a ripe old age is to avoid doctors and hospitals and learn about nutrition, herbal medicine and other forms of natural medicine unless you are fortunate enough to have a naturopathic physician available. Almost all drugs are toxic and are designed only to treat symptoms and not to cure anyone. Vaccines are highly dangerous, have never been adequately studied or proven to be effective, and have a poor risk/reward ratio. Most surgery is unnecessary and most textbooks of

medicine are inaccurate and deceptive. Almost every disease is said to be ideopathic (without known cause) or genetic - although this is untrue. In short, our mainstream medical system is hopelessly inept and/or corrupt. The treatment of cancer and degenerative diseases is a national scandal. The sooner you learn this, the better off you will be."

A. Greenburg, M.D.

Licensing

Earlier in the book I mentioned the insidious effect of Codex Alimentarius on taking our choices away and putting them into the hands of Big Corporate. This limiting of choice usually takes place via an officially sanctioned licensing system. A practitioner or manufacturer of foods or supplements must produce under a licence, within the guidelines of that license, or they will be 'struck off'. Often the requirements for that license are so complicated and expensive that small-scale operatives are unable to set-up in business or continue to operate if that already produce or apply 'treatments'. A fast and effective way to eliminate competition. So hundreds of herbal medicinal products are banned from sale in Britain under what campaigners say is a 'discriminatory and disproportionate European law'.

They do this through a system of licencing. The scam is simple: you introduce licences for something and then anyone who wants to do it must do it within your limits and restrictions or they don't get a licence and so cannot practice. If you want to stop people doing that 'something' you make the requirements to get a licence so complex and costly that you are, in effect, denying them the right to practice or produce.

They use this licencing technique throughout society to impose control and nowhere more so than in what passes for 'medicine'. A doctor needs a licence to practice and if they use healing methods that work, but are not recognised by the arbiters of the licence (ultimately Big Pharma) they lose their licence and are struck off.

The licencing noose is also being used ever more widely in alternative and complimentary medicine to install centralised control and dictatorship by a self-appointed authority. The major corporations have been buying up health store chains for years to kidnap the 'alternatives' industry.

It is still difficult to find definitives as to how the legislation actually works, it all seems so underhand. It seems under the radar of most people, it is a cynical way to make new laws that govern our choices. Some people think that the logical result of this is that even prescribing such things onion soup or peppermint tea as aids to health may become an illegal act because it is prescribing treatment without a license.

The new licensing system prescribes what is and isn't a 'treatment' to those acceptable by the corporations in control – effectively banning whole realms of, sometimes experimental, sometimes traditional, always inexpensive, interventions. Even the most common plants like nettle and garlic, and what a doctor can and can't do with them, come under this legislation.

At the same time, people are wising-up to the effectiveness of what were once called 'simples' in traditional folk medicine and their powers for health management. In the middle-ages in Europe the practitioners of this type of medicine were literally 'burnt at the stake' as part of social cleansing and religious persecution. This 'burning of the witches' robbed us of a truly important role, most often practised by women, of the local village healer, the hedgewitch. Simple, local, often food-based alteratives to help manage an ongoing state of health.

This aspect of our lives as self-healers is now controlled by the sometimes misplaced authority of doctors. Far too often they promote the products of big pharma over more simple remedies because if they don't, they are liable to be 'struck off' under their own licensing system for promoting unscientific, untested and unproven treatments. Yet no research into simple, readily available and natural cures is made because there is no profit in it for the big corporations.

Perhaps unwittingly this oppression opens the doors to two very important factors in a 'post-capitalist economy': mutuality and gardening. As people rediscover traditional techniques for growing and using plants in simple health management for themselves, they will not need the 'tainted' products of pharmaceutical industries. I hope that people will increasingly share their discoveries with each other using social media.

Many people are recognising that new legislation concerning food and health, under the guise of safety and harmonisation, is structured to limit our choices and access to natural foods and alternative medicines to profit Big Corporate.

Although licensing also affects the sale of seeds, it hasn't yet stopped the simple sharing of seed between people in social networks, although, already in some places like Tanzania, you can be imprisoned for this. Genetic manipulation has highly questionable and wholly unpredictable effects on nature but it hasn't yet reached the many wild and common plants at the heart of simple and effective remedies that can be grown even on the smallest windowsill, collected from the wild and made in a kitchen.

My hope is that Codex Alimentarius and similar 'trade agreements' will eventually have entirely the opposite effect intended by those who seek to exploit nature for personal profit. In the same way that *'every action has an equal and opposite reaction'*, many people, once they understand why their choices are being limited, will reclaim the responsibility for their own health from the profit motives of Big Pharma and a National Health Service that is really a National Sickness Service.

So far there is no legislation (that can be enforced) to stop people walking out to the countryside to pick wild plants – or to stop them growing and eating their own healthy foods and herbs at home, although Monsanto and other drug companies certainly have designs on changing this situation though bio-piracy.

New Medical Science

Doctor Kathy Sykes amongst others has presented us with scientific proof of how acupuncture and other meridian-based interventions might work. In what can only be described as a 'breakthrough experiment', she found visual evidence of the effect of acupuncture on the brain's limbic system, also known as the mammalian hind brain. Combining on-the-spot acupuncture with an MRI scanner she was able to view and record the direct effect of acupuncture on areas of the limbic brain.

Vibrational medicine, or energy medicine, attempts to treat people with various forms of energy. The influence of alternative medical systems such as Chinese, Ayervedic or Tibetan medicine have led in part to the development of machines that can image energy.

Heat energy imagers are an accepted part of our technology. We readily accept imaging heat, even though we can't see it, because heat is something we can sense through touch. With the 'energy body' it is not so straightforward. Very few of us have experienced this for ourselves and there is apparently no sensory backup, like holding out your hand in front of a source of heat, to tell us it is there.

Experiments in 'electro-acupuncture' and Kirlian photography have led to an energy map of the body identical to that shown in traditional Chinese medicine. The meridian system is seen as an interface between the physical body and the energy body. Applications of resonant energy to the meridian system promote healing in a number of dis-eases, by altering the energy of the root system concerned in the dis-ease. Much of this work seems to be undercover and information and the manufacture of equipment for treatments of this nature is actually suppressed through legislation.

The etheric body, acupuncture meridians, chakras and nadis and other multi-dimensional aspects of the human are described by ancient schools of healing throughout the world. Western medicine in its reductionist stance, ignores these aspects because they can't be studied under a microscope. Only now, at the beginning of the 21st century are some doctors starting to catch on.

Vibrational medicine interfaces with subtle energy fields that underly the functions of a physical body. It is based on the idea of resonant frequencies, similar to a tuned string on a musical instrument resonating with anything tuned to the same frequency, or an opera singer smashing a glass by singing at a certain pitch. Some sciences and philosophies have recognised vibrational elements as an important part of the universe. It is proving difficult to link these new sciences with the dogma of Western medicine. Even as long ago as 1928 Thomas Sugrue recognised vibrational elements at work in the human body, yet this story of the human being has remained mostly hidden:

"The human body is made up of electronic vibrations, with each atom and elements of the body, each organ and organism, having its electronic unit of vibration necessary for the sustenance of, and equilibrium in that particular

organism. Each unit, then, being a cell or a unit of life in itself has the capacity of reproducing itself by the first the law as is known as reproduction-division. When a force in any organ or element of the body becomes deficient in its ability to reproduce that equilibrium necessary for the sustenance of physical existence and its reproduction, that portion becomes deficient in electronic energy. This may come by injury or disease, received by external forces. It may come from internal forces through lack of eliminations produced in the system or by other agencies to meet its requirements in the body."

Edgar Cayce (1928) from ' *There is a River* 'by Thomas Sugrue.

Experiments in high-energy particle physics and the new field of quantum physics show us that nearly all matter is energy. In some sense we are made from 'frozen light'. As beings of energy we are influenced by and can be treated by energy and modern medicine is all too slowly realising this. For example early experiments by Toronto researchers have found that Alzheimer's patients showed temporary improvements in thinking skills and memory after sitting in a chair that pulsated with low-frequency sound vibrations of 40 hertz. This treatment, called rhythmic sensory stimulation, is to boost declining brain activity.

The Chinese are already combining the best of Western medicine to treat the effects of disease with the best of Eastern to treat the causes. Our medieval research methodologies in medicine mean that we are falling behind the Chinese in using a truly integrated medicine. There seem to be interested parties in our health care that have a vested interest in retaining expensive drugs and surgery as mainstream treatments.

Devices, and people, capable of sensing vibrations in a person are appearing but they make little sense to Western doctors. One such device uses simple voice analysis to identify missing frequencies in the sound of the voice. Practitioners are astounded at the accuracy of their findings and the speed of results in supplying the missing frequency to a patient. This tool is allowing switched-on energy workers to heal, unlike scientific Western medicine, without having to diagnose, because the treatment gets to the energy root problem directly. In some ways the effect of the illness is irrelevant - the principle is to replace the missing energies and allow the body to self-heal. This has always been the basis of Eastern healing philosophies. Taxing a patient with toxic drugs to treat the effect, as in allopathic medicine, can and often does cause more problems than it resolves. Although it makes a lot of money.

The Western narrative of health is misconstrued as a 'steady state'. In reality a healthy person is in a constant state of flux, of reacting to this environment, that foodstuff and so on. Health management is an ongoing event through ingesting food alteratives, herbs, drinks, exercise, meditation and sleep, exposure to environments and many other factors. To limit the story to 'ill or not ill' and to automatically hand-over to a doctor when ill is a simplification and an abdication of responsibility for your own body to an imagined 'authority', more of the slave mentality.

Government

Of course the government itself is one of the main control systems, bringing in legislation and laws that are often punitive to certain sorts of behaviour they don't want. Did you know that there are around 70 UK Government ministers with financial links to private health care firms? The NHS is already privatised!

Take for example the ridiculous legislation insisting that single mothers go out to work so that they can afford to pay for a child minder to look after their young. This unnatural and dehumanising process of separation is purely for the economic figures. It shows two people to be economically active where there were none; the mother in her poorly paid, part-time job and the carer she can't afford. The human 'cost' of this separation between mother and child doesn't even enter the equation.

The punitive effects of the Child Support Agency putting non-compliant parents out of their jobs with an 'attachment to earnings' is another example of legislation as social control and one I have experienced personally.

Woe betide you if you step outside the norms. The laws they create pick on the weak and the un-represented. The single mothers, the absent fathers, the 'extra bedroom' tax, the unemployed, the sick, the migrants driven from their homes by corporately sponsored bombs.

Legislation works hand-in-hand with media to first demonise, then tax minority groups making their lives even harder.

The situation gets even worse when the government make poorly contrived laws and then hand them on to private companies such as the infamous ATOS Work Capability Assessment in the UK. Linda Wooton, a 49 year old woman had undergone a double lung and heart transplant and was on 10 medications a day. Even though she was weak and suffering blackouts she was still put through the Work Capability Assessment. She received confirmation that she was fit for work as she lay in her hospital bed and died just nine days later.

Thanks to the Freedom of Information act, Iain Duncan Smith has been forced to release figures showing how many people declared fit for work by his department dropped dead.

More than 4,000 people died within six weeks of being found "fit for work", the Department for Work and Pensions has admitted. The figures cover the period between December 2011 to February 2014. All were told they should find a job following a "Work Capability Assessment".

Of the total, 1,360 died after losing an appeal against the decision. Apparently 80 people a week are dying after being assessed as fit for work. Now we know why Mr Duncan Smith and the Government were so reluctant to release these figures.

The absolute hypocrisy of politicians regarding this is unbelievable. Expenses scandals, second homes paid for by the taxpayers, cash for questions – all sorts of scams inhabit the world of our separated and privileged politicians. Take for example the bedroom tax – a tax made in the UK reducing benefit for people claiming out of work benefits who have more bedrooms than people in their house – and Jacob Rees Mogg, the Tory MP for North East Somerset. He voted for this tax on the poor whilst around the same time his wife's ancestral home received a £7.6 million 'state rescue'.

"The annual survey of public perceptions of Parliament commissioned by the Hansard Society - an independent charity that champions parliamentary democracy around the world. Over the last ten years or so it has charted the decline of Parliament's standing with the British public in forensic detail, through surveys of public opinion and through dispassionate analysis. It

leaves little to doubt. people think MP's are in it for themselves, cannot be trusted and do not understand ordinary people. Belief that our parliamentary system is 'fit for purpose' has fallen, so that only a quarter of people in Britain think it works well or only needs minor improvements."

Caroline Lucas

Education and Training

"Ideally, what should be said to every child, repeatedly, throughout his or her school life is something like this: 'You are in the process of being indoctrinated. We have not yet evolved a system of education that is not a system of indoctrination. We are sorry, but it is the best we can do. What you are being taught here is an amalgam of current prejudice and the choices of this particular culture. The slightest look at history will show how impermanent these must be. You are being taught by people who have been able to accommodate themselves to a regime of thought laid down by their predecessors. It is a self-perpetuating system. Those of you who are more robust and individual than others will be encouraged to leave and find ways of educating yourself, educating your own judgements. Those that stay must remember, always, and all the time, that they are being moulded and patterned to fit into the narrow and particular needs of this particular society."

Doris Lessing

Another 'myth making machine and social control institution' is the education system. Our education system is failing both our children and adults. It has become so focused on 'economic outcomes' that we have forgotten what education is actually for. We are spending all our resources on teaching people what to think when we should be teaching them how to think for themselves.

Hegemony in education

Our educational system is presently lost. Education has largely been replaced by systems of indoctrination. Just how has this come about?

"An educational system which exclusively aims to transform people into commodities for consumption on the labour market must treat them in turn

as passive consumers. The curriculum will consist of objects to be possessed in the form of facts and skills rather than objects of thought: situations, problems and issues which are capable of challenging, activating and extending natural powers of being".

Eliot J. Action Research for Educational Change. OU Press 1992.

So where has the system become lost? Why is the educational system still based around 'the transmission of knowledge'? Knowles gives us a historical context for 'pedagogic transmission'. He states the Greeks invented 'Socratic dialogue' as an aid to learning, where a member of the group would pose a question to be explored by the 'group mind'. The Romans were more confrontational and developed polarities in argument which we can still see in our political and educational systems today. In limiting options to pro's and con's, left and right, black and white, in or out (Brexit), Republican or Democrat, we keep people in conflict.

"Starting in the seventh century in Europe, schools began being organised for teaching children, primarily for preparing young boys for the priesthood, hence they became known as cathedral or monastic schools. Since the teachers in these schools had as their principal mission the indoctrination of students in the beliefs, faiths and rituals of the Church, they evolved a set of assumptions about learning and strategies for teaching that came to be labelled as 'pedagogy'...This model of education persisted through the ages ... and was the basis of organisation of our entire educational system".

Knowles M. The Adult Learner, A Neglected Species. Gulf. 1990.

It saddens me that the following extract from Lindemann (found in Knowles) was written as long ago as 1926:

"We shall never know how many adults desire intelligence regarding themselves and the world in which they live until education once more escapes the pattern of conformity. Adult education is an attempt to discover a new method and create a new incentive for learning; its implications are qualitative not quantitative. Adult learners are precisely those whose intellectual aspirations are least likely to be aroused by the rigid, uncompromising requirements of authoritative, conventionalized institutions of learning".

Lindeman E.C. The Meaning of Adult Education. in Knowles.

No wonder so many people are put off education at an early age.

David Icke, much ridiculed because of his far-fetched claims, asserts in his book '*The Robot's Rebellion*', that the system has no intention of educating people, it exists to turn out fodder for the system, 'to become the next generation of robots'. Although great teachers exist within the system and attempt to lessen the indoctrination, they are subject to the limitations of increasing government control.

"This is their [the government's] way of finding some illusion of security in a mythical 1950's utopia in which everyone had their place and everyone knew what it was. This back to basics policy when applied to education, puts an emphasis on 'talking at' teaching, and expansion of tests and exams and, to quote one former Education Secretary, a return to teaching a fear of God. Give me strength".

Icke D. The Robot's Rebellion, The Story of the Spiritual Renaissance. Gateway Books 1994.

As the government once again take control of our curriculum for an 'upgrade' many teachers must be considering whether it will be worth all of the effort. But now more than ever we need our education systems to turn out non-conformists who are able to think for themselves and create real alternatives. They need to question the irrational values of corporate consumer capitalism and find alternatives that actually work and they are not being given even the most basic tools to do this.

Cut and Paste Education

"Some say I should be in school, but why should any young person be made to study for a future when no one is doing enough to save that future? What is the point of learning facts when the most important facts given by the finest scientists are ignored by our politicians?"

Greta Thunberg, 15 year old Swedish student.

Cutting and pasting essays from the internet is a wholly rational response to an education system that is now an indoctrination system. The word 'education' has its origins in the root word 'educare' – meaning to 'draw out and extend'. Modern education no longer does this. It imposes a curriculum on students that has its basis in making us look economically superior to the Germans. The purposes for modern mainstream education are built around economic objectives and are not about the development of human beings as individuals, their potential, values and identity in a changing world. Real education starts where you are – it is grounded in real, personal and lived experience. Real education gives you the tools to reflect on your own experience and make your own sense of it. It helps you to adapt to a new reality in the face of changing circumstances.

In contrast to this, much of our modern education is remote and distant from the real experience of students. It consists of predetermined material, often with extreme bias, which is tested by processes of examination, one of which is writing essays. Successful schools and colleges are now little more than 'exam factories', their main focus geared towards turning out the maximum amount of qualifications to secure future funding from the government.

A focus on industrial outputs has destroyed education in this country. In reality about 60% of the information we will need as individuals this time next year, does not yet exist. Yet we are still imposing on, rather than listening to our students. Where are the skills of learning how to learn in the curriculum, the skills of creativity, adaptability and versatility? Where are the skills of self-maintenance, of invention, innovation and self-motivation? They don't seem to be required in an 'education' system that seeks conformity. These are essential skills for an economy that is now essentially bankrupt. These are the skills our children will need for the 21st Century. We are imposing useless indoctrination on our students that has little to do with their lives and even less to do with the future we have made for them. Nearly everything we are imposing on our children through a government imposed curriculum, is a preparation for a future that no longer exists. It is no wonder truancy rates in the UK are the highest ever.

Many of the students recognize this. They see schools and colleges as hurdles they have to jump on the 'way to a life' their parents don't seem to be questioning. They know, at a diversity of levels, from 'an uneasy feeling' (cognitive dissonance) to real political insight, that most of what they are 'taught' is useless in the context of an economic system that is doomed to failure for committing the idiocy of using its capital assets as income.

The students on the whole know that teachers and lecturers are so busy and stressed with the system that they don't have a hope in hell of catching them cutting and pasting their studies. They want to get on with living their own lives, where in fact they learn far more than they do in the sterile centers of indoctrination and imposed conformity that our schools and colleges have become.

Current theory suggests that regurgitating material from one place on the internet is regarded as 'plagiarism' but copying from ten is 'research'. This is nitpicking when the whole concept of how we learn and the whole technology of learning has so radically shifted. Cut and paste is a rational response to a system that keeps on regurgitating the same old stuff in a reality that has utterly changed.

Spectator Sport

The narratives of oppositionalism extend also to sport. Right from School Sports Day we are taught that competition is a good thing, that winning is better than helping. The 'us and them' of football teams, the nationalism of being 'proud to be English', black or white, local or newcomer, tory or labour, democrat or republican, us or them creates a world divided. TV programs where individuals or teams are set against each other all endorse 'winning' as the prime goal. Some sports like tennis are clearly gladiatorial, one opponent pitted against another in an Romanesque ampitheatre. Many of our Olympic Games are based on military practices for men.

When we set people against each other in competitions or contests we ask them to confuse excellence with winning, as if the only way to do something well is to out-do the others. We encourage them to measure their own value in terms of how many people they have beaten, which is not exactly a path to mental health.

They see their fellow competitors not as potential friends or collaborators but as obstacles to their own success. It leads people to regard whatever they are doing as a means to an end. It prevents us from finding and recognising excellence for its own value. It devalues what we do when we set out to 'win'. Once you get caught-up in the idea that 'winning' is the point, you risk losing decency, integrity, fairness, compassion and humility. This is the competitive environment fostered by corporate capitalism and the basis on which both the UK and the US has chosen its national leaders.

Just forget the fact that the military basis of the Olympic sports are contrived to exclude women from fair competition with men. There is no gender parity here and only in a very few of the sports are men and women included together. Make no mistake, more women in the Olympics is a step forward, but this is physical competition in a man's terms.

One wonders, if Olympic sports were something that changed with the times, what could be included that might promote gender parity. Perhaps games that include strategy, cunning, cooperation like working together at solving problems.

The Olympics are a tribute to the sponsorship and shameless promotion of corporate power in general. What on earth do Coca Cola, McDonalds and many of the other fifty or so partners, supporters, suppliers and providers have to do with the tradition of human excellence in sport? Coca Cola are the longest continuous sponsor of the Olympic movement. They see their role as official soft drinks provider enables them to showcase the range of drinks they offer and sell these at the Olympic and Paralympic Games.

Their sugar or chemical-filled drinks have obviously not helped many of the sports people attain their brilliance, along with McDonalds who have obviously (not) fed them all to nutritional peaks of achievement. Is it just me feeling uneasy that these two companies are major 'partners' in the Olympics? Is it with some sense of irony that they have become sponsors?

In addition to its promotion of corporate power as something acceptable and unquestionable, the Olympic Games promote a concept of privilege that is central to the class system in the United Kingdom. The Class system is an archaic system based on status and rewards which is well past its 'best by' date. The whole method of purchasing and distribution of tickets serves to promote 'prestige' and fictions about 'reward' so prevalent to driving consumer capitalism.

As for petty nationalism, please do not include me. Although I live in the UK, I am a Citizen of the World and dislike the whole 'us and them' scenario promoted by these games, because, in the end, there is only us, there is no them. "We beat Brazil," you claim. "Not me mate. I did nothing and it seems to me that your part in it was pretty infinitesimal because you give every appearance of somebody sitting on the sofa making sports noises."

And there's another thing. Why do we have to be endlessly patronized by sports commentators shouting at us as if they are excited children on a sugar hit? Is it compulsory for them to drink the sugary drinks provided by sponsors so that they can 'go off into one'? The whole hyped-up way of talking over-excitedly when there is clearly very little actually happening is just sensory pollution of the worst kind. Its like trying to appreciate a glass of wine by drinking somebody else's puke.

The Olympics do provide a great spectacle and distraction from the latest War in Syria, the Great Eurozone Sham, Brexit, the Global Debt Crisis and our Environment Spiralling into Chaos. But petty nationalism through sport is a form of denial and a means to continue to ignore Climate Chaos, the Genocide of Amazonians and all the other things we don't want to think about.

The original meaning of the word 'competition' means 'striving together'. Somewhere in the mists of time this has been lost and the Olympics provide a spectacle of nations striving against each other to win – what? Big, Fat Gold Coins, a symbol of 'money', the very problem at the heart of our downfall.

Darwinian fictions about 'survival of the fittest' drive the competitions. Where do we have nations striving together to achieve something beyond beating their opponents? Where are we shown that 'co-operation' between individuals or teams is the most desirable trait of a lead species? It would certainly not seem to be in the Olympics, a tale of victory, winning, nationalism and a massive corporate lie.

Marriage, Families and Sexuality

A family is the traditional system that benefits consumerism the most. And hereby hangs another tale. Every family will need a house, full of consumer durables like washing machines and fridges and cars which they only use for part of the time. They will often have to pay for childcare services for when they go to work or go out. Each individual living space requires heating and lighting, water & waste disposal services, phones and so on, often provided by a central monopoly for a building often designed to squander these precious resources through inefficiency.

A book by Daniel Pinchbeck, called *'How Soon is Now?'* describes perfectly the limitations of modern relationships and other possibilities that few of us seem to question. It shows how many of the stories embedded in the socioeconomic unit of the family are flawed. I have edited his sample chapter down.

"Unconsciously, we have been impelling ourselves towards planetary catastrophe. I believe we are doing this to end our alienation and ego-centrism – to reach a new intensity of communion. Because we no longer have rites of passage which create the same effect through intentionally guided ritual, we are inducing it through mass catastrophe. But the disasters we are unleashing could have the unanticipated effect of breaking open the collective heart chakra. Collectively, humanity can realize love and solidarity – universal, unconditional – as the basis for healing our world.

This may seem distant, theoretical and abstract, but I think many people already see reverberations of this process in their personal lives. For some, this is taking the form of a deep questioning of traditional relationship patterns – often, a rejection of them, as they seek to create something new. Culturally, the focus on transgendered people, gay marriage, the endless sex scandals tearing down politicians and public figures is all part of this unavoidable change.

We have inherited a restricted model of romantic and erotic love. Most people still believe that monogamy – exclusive partnership – is the only way to enduring happiness and contentment. Of course, for some people, monogamy is the best option. But humans are not naturally monogamous, and the current system forces many people to act hypocritically, to deceive themselves and their partners, or to sacrifice their truth.

Deep in their hearts, many people feel permanently disappointed, sad, frustrated and angry because they have been unable to satisfy their erotic desires. Men and women lead lives of quiet desperation and compromise. An ambience of disappointment and frustration permeates our society, in overt and subtle ways. People seek false substitutes for true satisfaction. The insatiable lust for consumer goods is – I believe – a result of our failure to satisfy our deeper needs for love, erotic fulfilment, authentic communion.

'We are at war with our eroticism', write Christopher Ryan and Calcida Jethá in '*Sex at Dawn: The Prehistoric Origins of Modern Sexuality*'. After scouring evidence from anthropology and evolutionary biology, they point out that, Human beings evolved in intimate groups where almost every-thing was shared – food, shelter, protection, child care, even sexual pleasure . . . contemporary culture misrepresents the link between love and sex. With and without love, a casual sexuality was the norm for our prehistoric ancestors . . . human beings and our hominid ancestors have spent almost all of the past million years or so in small, intimate bands in which most adults had several sexual relationships at any given time.

Civilization constructed the institution of marriage, and enforced monogamy, to protect property rights, under a patriarchal regime which demonized female sexuality. The force of our repressed sexual instinct was channeled – or sublimated, in Sigmund Freud's term – into building civilisation, creating culture and making war.

The curious fact about human nature is that it is not fixed, but changeable. This is something that makes us different from animals: we are the species that can reinvent itself, in many ways. However, some things are very resistant to change. The instinct towards sexual satiation, for instance, is hardwired into our biology. We are also unique among animals due to the incessant force of our non-stop, hair-trigger sex drive.

As Gerald Heard explored in the early 1950s in '*Pain, Sex and Time*', we possess a tremendous surplus of evolutionary energy, far beyond what we need to sustain ourselves. This energy must find outlets for expression. Like Walter Benjamin, Heard believed we need to channel this force consciously, through ritual, initiation and training in special schools devised for this purpose. Otherwise, the excess energy continues to get discharged, through wars and violence.

'If our evolution is over,' Heard worried, 'if we have no further original outlet to our enormous and fretting energy, then the only choice is slow degeneracy through sex addiction or a conclusive end through homicidal mania.' The excess energy, the kundalini, driving us reveals something important about our destiny as a species. In other words, individually as well as collectively, we can choose to evolve and deepen ourselves, or decay and disintegrate.

Sex energy radiates through every lament of our social structure. 'Sexuality is a superpower,' writes Dieter Duhm, one of the founders of Tamera, a 'free love' community in Portugal. 'Our attractions and repulsions, sexual signals and links, hopes and disappointments go through all of society like a nerve system, permeating every office, every shopping mall, every art exhibition, every conference, every group, every company, every political party.' He believes that any attempt to suppress this superpower only leads to negative outcomes – as with those Indian gurus in the 1970s who claimed to be transcendent masters, but couldn't resist the charms of their Western female disciples.

Duhm was the leader of a group of German radicals who tried to understand why 1960s leftist efforts to build a utopian alternative to capitalism ended in failure. He realized there were core issues around love, relationships and sexuality that people could not fully address yet or bring into their consciousness. 'The healing of sexuality is perhaps the most revolutionary step in the present healing work after thousands of years of suppression and neglect,' he writes. Because these issues were not addressed, the idealistic efforts to change the world imploded, instead. Communities and movements kept falling apart. Sex and love were the deepest political issues society could not confront or integrate.

'The most intimate questions of sex, love, and partnership, of faithfulness, trust, and community, of jealousy, competition, and fear of separation are political questions with global implications', Duhm writes. He and some like-minded people decided to step out of society to establish a community as an experimental laboratory. Their modest goal was world peace. They realized that peace on Earth would be impossible until we established peace between the genders – until we found peace in love. They courageously broke apart traditional structures and conditioning, seeking a holistic redesign.

I remember from my early years, my adolescence, how the cultural ambience around sexuality had a dark, shameful feeling. There was no sense that boys and girls – or men and women – might seek to collaborate for each other's sensual pleasure. That we might enjoy taking care of each other – that we could learn to be generous, compassionate, with each other. Eroticism was not part of our education. It was not something to be explored or studied, even as an afterthought – certainly not with the same kind of analytic rigour we brought to maths or physics, even though sex would be infinitely more important to our future lives than these academic subjects.

Our civilization applies tremendous reserves of intellect and capital to construct killer drones, virtual reality devices, surveillance systems – instruments of death, alienation and fear. Yet we believe that love and sexuality are not worthy of our conscious attention. We act as if they are outside the realm of logic, forethought and social design.

'Whereas the cerebrum is applied in war technology, in love man lives and thinks out of his spinal cord,' Duhm points out. When we channel more of society's intellect and resources towards the exploration of love and eroticism – freeing these areas from an antiquated and unrealistic morality – we will make rapid strides.

Just as we lack rites of passage to introduce us to transpersonal or visionary experiences when we are young – when we long, with our whole being, to experience a deeper intensity of communion, to access something greater than ourselves – we also lack for cultural traditions that would help young people to embrace their sexuality as something wonderful, as a great gift they can explore and share responsibly. We are still a subtly pleasure-denying society, despite Tinder, OkCupid, casual sex and the hook-up culture. Sexuality is considered a private matter, relegated to dark places like nightclubs and bars, which have an underworld ambience.

Sexual hunger is quite different from the hunger for food, which is easily satisfied by a good meal, or even a mediocre buffet. Russell Brand became a raging sex addict who slept with up to eighty women a month at the height of his mania, or so he claims. Not only is Russell extremely charming and charismatic, he would also enlist people to help him in his quest to be 'shagger of the year', a title he held several times in a row. Eventually, he realized that this almost unbelievable expenditure of sweat and sperm was bringing him no lasting contentment, so he checked into rehab.

Russell may have gone a bit overboard. But my admittedly controversial perspective is that there is nothing wrong with having an abundance, even a super-abundance, of lovers and sexual partners –

whether for men or women – as long as this is done honestly and without coercion. Unfortunately, in our society, the pursuit of sexual desire tends to require all sorts of miserable deceits, lies and hypocrisies. Also, it is totally unjust and wrong that women still get put down for the exact same behavior that society approves in men.

I suspect some readers will feel I am promoting a hyper-masculine mode of sexuality. Of course, men are more biologically prone to seek multiple mates, but women also have the need to pursue various sorts of erotic adventures. In '*Sex at Dawn*', Ryan and Jethá review studies that suggest there is an evolutionary explanation for why women make louder sounds during intercourse than men. These noises had a function in our early hominid days: the female was calling out to other males in the area to have sex with her in succession. In this way, the child's paternity would remain unknown. Also, sperm competition would occur in the uterus. The female orgasm also has a reproductive purpose, as the contractions of orgasm pull the sperm deeper into the womb. The male who elicited the most powerful orgasm would be the one most likely to fertilize her egg.

When it comes to sexuality, we have to accept how humans truly are, rather than how they are supposed to be, according to some imposed ideal. 'Monogamy is not found in any social, group-living primate except – if the standard narrative is to be believed – us,' write Ryan and Jethá:

If you spend time with the primates closest to human beings, you'll see female chimps having intercourse dozens of times per day, with most or all of the willing males, and rampant bonobo group sex that leaves everyone relaxed and maintains intricate social networks. Explore contemporary human beings' lust for particular kinds of pornography or our notorious difficulties with long-term sexual monogamy and you'll soon stumble over relics of our hypersexual ancestors.

The planetary mega-crisis is directly related to the problems we confront as a species in this area of love and sexuality. One primary urge driving many men to seek success – wealth or fame – is sexual access. Men – Alpha males, in particular – will do almost anything to attract women. The economic system tends to reward sociopathic behaviour. To succeed, people must climb corporate ladders, sell wasteful products, manage investment funds that transfer resources from the poor to the wealthy, promote vacuous fashion trends and so on. The system forces people to compromise their ethics and principles, or renounce them altogether, to get what they want.

My anthropological observation is that people – young people above all – waste an unbelievable amount of their life energy in the quest for sexual satiation. This energy that people expend in the incessant pursuit of sexual fulfilment is exactly the energy that we, the human community, need to redirect, channeling it towards our awakening, using it to enact social change and regenerate our planet's ecosystems.

Sex itself is not the problem. In our culture, for many people, the act of sex only consumes a tiny fraction of the energy expended in the pursuit of it. Also, sex can be nourishing, physically and emotionally. If there was no need to pursue erotic connections, to compete for mates, we could use that squandered energy to confront the ecological crisis we have unleashed as a species, and bring about a rapid cultural evolution.

If we can understand, and then fix, the flaws in our social design, our stale ideology and antiquated cultural programming, we will liberate a huge amount of productive energy for building a regenerative society. We will take a massive leap forward as a species. And we will do it quickly.

I don't think the answer is to restrict sexual behaviour, which will only lead to more frustration, repression, resentment and deception. I believe the solution is to consciously liberate Eros – not just Eros as it gets expressed through sexuality and romantic love, but also the various forms of love that bind communities together, including caring for children and old people. We must understand that the Eros that gets expressed through sexuality is not just an individual problem, but has a very large-scale social and political dimension. Men and women must be willing to cooperate for each other's happiness if humanity is going to have a long-term future on Earth.

Hollywood and the media idealize the nuclear family, which is the basic economic unit of our society. When individuals merge into couples, and particularly when these couples have children, they tend to direct all their energy and resources towards themselves. They lose interest – if they ever had any – in helping the collective. Instead, they seek to amass resources, playing the competitive capitalist game.

The problem in our culture is the atomization which forces individuals, as well as nuclear families, to fight for their own success and personal survival. We can now see that this system, enforcing self- interest as a survival mechanism, is not sustainable for the planet as a whole. It needs to change – since it won't change on its own, we need to change it.

'Deep conflicts rage at the heart of modern sexuality,' write Ryan and Jethá: Our cultivated ignorance is devastating. The campaign to obscure the true nature of our species' sexuality leaves half our marriages collapsing under an unstoppable tide of sexual frustration, libido-killing boredom, impulsive betrayal, dysfunction, confusion, and shame. Serial monogamy stretches before (and behind) many of us like an archipelago of failure: isolated islands of transitory happiness in a cold, dark sea of disappointment.

To maintain their relationships, many people find themselves forced to lie about or suppress their true desires. The vast majority of men I know who are in long-term partnerships have confessed they either feel an intense desire for other sexual contacts or have secretly satisfied some of those desires, through affairs or prostitutes – feeding the horrific global sex trade. Other people learn to dampen their sexual drive, but I don't find this a great outcome either.

I don't think it is an accident that so many creative artists and geniuses have been fascinated with eroticism and sexual love, pursuing the muse as she expresses herself in many embodied forms. Erotic love is a kind of fuel that makes people feel alive and inspired. Ideally, don't we want everyone to be as inspired and turned-on as they can be? Wouldn't we prefer a social system that supports everyone in exploring their deepest capacities for love, for erotic and ecstatic experience, as long as they are causing no harm to others?

There is a direct relationship between our corrupt politics and our failure, as a society, to handle love authentically. When people find themselves forced to lie to or deceive the person closest to them – their partner – about their desires, they are conditioned to accept corruption and hypocrisy in society at large. They can accept the half-truths of politicians and pundits because they are compromised themselves. We fail to care for the world as a consequence of our inauthenticity. After all, why would we want to protect and safeguard a world that has betrayed us at its core?

Taken from the sample chapter of a new book by Daniel Pinchbeck, called 'How Soon is Now?' available from http://howsoonisnow.info/

This article was found at: http://www.ecohustler.co.uk /2017/01/29/sexuality-superpower-can-unleashed-heal-world/

4. THE BREAKDOWN

"Human domination over nature is quite simply an illusion, a passing dream by a naive species. It is an illusion that has cost us much, ensnared us in our own designs, given us a few boasts to make about our courage and genius, but all the same it is an illusion."

Donald Worster

"The apocalpse is not something which is coming. The apocalypse has arrived in major portions of the planet and it's only because we live within a bubble of incredible privilege and social insulation that we still have the luxury of anticipating the apocalypse."

Terrence Mckenna

Since we seem so committed to it, what are likely outcomes in the breakdown of our culture and socioeconomic system? From Tom McKay.

"Civilization was pretty great while it lasted, wasn't it? Too bad it's not going to for much longer. According to a new study sponsored by NASA's Goddard Space Flight Center, we only have a few decades left before everything we know and hold dear collapses. According to 'Extinction Rebellion', we have just 12 years to make the necessary changes, and some say even less than that. Already, a 2 metre sea level rise looks fairly certain. Science will surely save us, the nay-sayers may yell. But technology, argues Motesharrei, has only damned us further.

Technological change can raise the efficiency of resource use, but it also tends to raise both per capita resource consumption and the scale of resource extraction, so that, absent policy effects, the increases in consumption often compensate for the increased efficiency of resource use.

In other words, the benefits of technology are outweighed by how much the gains reinforce the existing, over-burdened system making collapse even more likely.

The worst-case scenarios predicted by Motesharrei are pretty dire, involving sudden collapse due to famine or a drawn-out breakdown of society due to the over-consumption of natural resources. The best-case scenario involves recognition of the looming catastrophe by Elites and a more equitable restructuring of society, but who really believes that is going to happen? Here's what the study recommends in a nutshell:

The two key solutions are to reduce economic inequality so as to ensure fairer distribution of resources, and to dramatically reduce resource consumption by relying on less intensive renewable resources and reducing population growth.

These are great suggestions that will, unfortunately, almost certainly never be put into action, considering just how far down the wrong path our civilization has gone. As of last year, humans are using more resources than the Earth can replenish and the planet's distribution of resources among its terrestrial inhabitants is massively unequal. This is what happened to Rome and the Mayans, according to the report.

'… *historical collapses were allowed to occur by elites who appear to be oblivious to the catastrophic trajectory'* (most clearly apparent in the Roman and Mayan cases).

And that's not even counting the spectre of global climate change, which could be a looming 'instant planetary emergency.' According to Canadian Wildlife Service biologist Neil Dawe:

"Economic growth is the biggest destroyer of the ecology. Those people who think you can have a growing economy and a healthy environment are wrong. If we don't reduce our numbers, nature will do it for us … Everything is worse and we're still doing the same things. Because ecosystems are so resilient, they don't exact immediate punishment on the stupid".

In maybe the nicest way to say the end is nigh possible, Motesharrei's report concludes that *"closely reflecting the reality of the world today … we find that collapse is difficult to avoid."*

Writes Nafeez Ahmed at The Guardian:

"Although the study is largely theoretical, a number of other more empirically-focused studies — by KPMG and the UK Government Office of Science for instance — have warned that the convergence of food, water and energy crises could create a 'perfect storm' within about fifteen years. But these 'business as usual' forecasts could be very conservative."

Article written by Tom McKay of www.policymic.com

Guido Dalla Casa writing for LTEconomy spells it out:

"There are 76 billion people on the earth with a 90 million people increase every year. Every year $100,000 km^2$ of forest disappears, CO_2 concentration in the atmosphere increases at 3ppm year after year, 30-40 species go extinct every day...clearly these phenomena, a consequence of the economic growth ideology, cannot continue much longer".

Tipping Points

Henry Cloud wrote:

"We change our behaviour when the pain of staying the same becomes greater than the pain of changing. Consequences give us the pain that motivates us to change".

Unfortunately there appears to be a thirty to sixty year delay on facing the consequences of our actions in using up the planet as if it were just here for our convenience. So it seems certain that not enough people are going to change their ways in time to avert environmental disasters of catastrophic proportions. In the meantime one of Trump's first moves was to remove all references to climate change and global warming from the Whitehouse website because to the mind of a malignant narcissist, this is all you have to do to make the problem go away.

Our present governments are powerless to do anything from within the socio-economic system we have – from their position of deep within the pocket of the profit motive. The economic values of humankind are incompatible with the laws of nature. The cult of material consumerism has a different story to the trees, the birds and the bees – and it doesn't include them. The mass extinction has already begun.

Some of us realize this, but not enough to make any real difference. Even if everyone in the UK became carbon neutral overnight it would take China just a couple of months to make up the footprint size. To compound the catastrophe, the effects of global warming are being temporarily hidden in the oceans, which seem to be acting as a great sponge, soaking up the heat for a short while. The complexity and interrelated nature of the issues is mostly too much for people who just want to get on with going to work, earning a living, paying their mortgages, bringing up their children and watching Strictly or X Factor.

Consensus amongst scientists seems to be that the 'tipping point' has already passed. The National Oceanic and Atmospheric Administration says the amount of heat-trapping carbon dioxide in the atmosphere has topped 400 parts per million. The 400 ppm threshold has been an important marker in U.N. climate change negotiations, widely recognized as a dangerous level that could drastically worsen human-caused global warming. The Scientific American claims that *"sudden, irreversible changes in the relatively stable conditions that have allowed civilization to flourish,"* are increasingly likely. Human nature shows that many people won't believe it even after it has happened.

There are plans for technical fixes of giant proportions, such as spraying the sky with a reflective layer to diminish the radiation from the sun to compensate. Conspiracy theorists assert that experiments have already begun, using military and commercial aircraft to spray barium, nano-aluminum-coated fiberglass, radioactive thorium, cadmium, chromium, nickel, desiccated blood, mold spores, yellow fungal mycotoxins, ethylene dibromide, and polymer fibres into the atmosphere. Some even attribute more sinister intentions to this airborne cocktail. Many scientists and authorities deny that there is evidence for any of it. Once again the truth is obscured.

Geo-engineering, cloud-seeding ships, space mirrors or even just planting more trees are all possible techno fixes to an escalating problem (meanwhile we still continue to cut down 5.2 million hectares of forest globally per year).

One solution to the problem seems obvious – use less energy – but this is not compatible with economies based on 'growth', as they increasingly fail to meet energy reduction targets or who, like Canada, 'opt out' of the climate agreements they have already made. Perhaps technical fixes will be helpful in the short term – but their effects are completely unpredictable and un-researched. As with many human meddling attempts to improve nature, it may well do more harm than good.

For some of our future-seers, it is already too late to make a difference. Former deputy editor of the Ecologist, Paul Kingsnorth became disillusioned with a fragmented and ineffective green movement and sees:

"The failure of humanity to respond to the crises it has created becomes increasingly obvious. Together we are able to say it loud and clear: we are not going to 'save the planet'. The planet is not ours to save. The planet is not dying; but our civilisation might be, and neither green technology nor ethical shopping is going to prevent a serious crash."

Many people have joined him and the other founders of the Dark Mountain project, to create more honest stories for a civilization in terminal decline. It seems that humans are chromosomally programmed to self-destruct. As Thomas Berry wrote:

"the devastation of the earth appears to be our destiny."

This puts a lot of pressure on us poor little humans who, having climbed-up from protozoic slime so quickly – seem to have landed on a snake and have to slide down to start again – if we survive at all. But perhaps there are reasons for this.

There is a huge flaw at the heart of Western Civilisation – the dualism of heart and mind, physic and spirit, body and soul – brought about through the philosophies stemming from Cartesian Dualism. These essentially separate us from nature and have created a basis for the illusions that the conditions of modern life are in any way desirable or durable.

It seems to me that within the pressure barrel of modern society there are more and more people 'evolving', discovering a higher purpose beyond our mundane material existence on this earth. People are moving into the third paradigm and are discovering for themselves a whole relationship with themselves, each other, wild nature and environment beyond a subsistence existence. Perhaps this is the very reason this 'pressure' exists? Just now, right now, there is a window of about 10 years or so where those people lucky enough to have their basic needs fulfilled might be on the ascendant to a completely new way of being, if the planet doesn't shift us all into chaos.

Maybe the choice is that simple: extinction or transcendence, the pressure of our imminent extinction being here to push as many into transcendence as possible. It wouldn't be the first time the dominant life form on this planet has been wiped out in preference to another.

There are at least two tipping points at work here. The first is that 'Nature Bats Last' and the majority of people are not going to do anything about the incoming environmental catastrophes until they have to – by which time it is too late. Once they see the size of 'Nature's Bat', they will want to act but it will already be 30 years too late.

The other tipping point is that of evolving people, the 100th Monkey Effect. Researchers at Rensselaer Polytechnic Institute have found that when just 10% of the population holds an unshakeable belief, their belief will always be adapted by the majority of their society. The scientists used computational and analytical methods to discover the tipping point where a minority belief becomes the majority opinion. The finding has implications for the study and influence of societal interactions ranging from the spread of innovations to the movement of political ideas. When the number of committed opinion holders is below 10% there is no visible progress in the spread of ideas. Once that number grows above 10% the idea spreads like flames.

The race is on.

The Cycles of Nature

In nature, nothing is wasted. Leaves, excess fruit, even wild animals who have died, leech back into the ground to fertilise it, creating perfect cycles like that of sun and rain, day and night, summer and winter.

Our economy, managed by government and seemingly their 'raison d'être', thrives on waste and built-in obsolescence. It wastes materials and resources in creating incredibly inefficient machines and tons of health destroying plastic. It wastes and exploits its people. It produces mountains of toxic rubbish polluting the earth until the end of time. Some people say that the effect of the economy is to dig stuff out of holes on one side of the planet, then put it back into different holes on the other side, destroying the local environment each time. The actions of the Myth of Economics poison the skies, the rivers, streams and oceans to feed the emptiness of the 'hungry ghosts' it breeds in order to line the pockets of the wealthy wetiko's.

Our economy destroys peoples' lives and keeps them enslaved and ignorant, spending their time in empty and meaningless activities, finding distraction only in leisure activities that once again serve the economic system.

The system has become a monster, a leviathan, trundling its way towards a precipice of environmental breakdown. And yet there is still no realistic option than to vote for just another aspect of the shadow puppets who service its machinery.

Life on Earth though, has been polluted before. In a book by James Lovelock, '*Gaia, A New Look at Life on Earth*' he provides one example of total global pollution that has already occurred on Planet Earth. The prevalent life-form two aeons ago were 'anaerobes', organisms that can only grow in the absence of oxygen. The release of oxygen gas into the early atmosphere was "*the worst atmospheric pollution incident that this planet has ever known.*" Although it resulted in a 'mass-extinction event', it also heralded the beginning of oxygen breathing life forms. Hence:

"*Ingenuity triumphed and the danger was overcome, not in the human way by restoring the old order, but in the flexible Gaian way by adapting to change and converting a murderous intruder into a powerful friend.*"

Civilisations have fallen before. The mysteries of Easter Island and the Rapa Nui, the invincible Mayans whose cities emptied over the space of a few years, The Roman Empire are three examples. Nature seems to have cycles of abundance, followed by destruction and rebirth. Nothing stays the same – change is the only constant.

A report, written by applied mathematician Safa Motesharrei of the National Socio-Environmental Synthesis Center along with a team of natural and social scientists, explains how our modern civilization is doomed. Apparently the entire fundamental structure and nature of our society is at fault.

The report analyses five risk factors for societal collapse. These are:

- population
- climate
- water
- agriculture
- energy

When these factors converge to form two important criteria the report says that the sudden downfall of complicated societal structures can follow. All societal collapses over the past 5,000 years have involved both *"the stretching of resources due to the strain placed on the ecological carrying capacity"* and *"the economic stratification of society into Elites and Masses"* This 'Elite' population restricts the flow of resources accessible to the 'Masses', accumulating a surplus for themselves that is high enough to strain natural resources. This situation will inevitably result in the destruction of society.

Elite power, the report suggests, will buffer 'detrimental effects of the environmental collapse until much later than the Commoners,' allowing the privileged to "continue 'business as usual' despite the impending catastrophe."

There are a number of choices we can make when faced with the meltdown of our culture. Perhaps it is a good thing, after all, despite its brilliant attainments, because aspects of our 'civilisation' are exceptionally cruel. Those of us who can see what is going on, who see the battle between the 'wetikos', earthbound, cannibalistic materialists without any connection to the whole, and those of us who wish to fulfil our potential as humans, what do we do?

'Be the change you want to see in the world' (inaccurately ascribed to Ghandi) is not enough. Surely the greedy ones will just keep taking until there is not enough for anyone. If you want to act (and most people won't), then some kind of resistance might be in order?

So what are the reactions beyond being frozen to the spot and doing nothing – which, unfortunately is what most people will do whilst they wait to be led?

Figure 3: Sculpture by street artist Isaac Cordal titled 'Politicians Debating Global Warming.'

5. FIGHT OR FLIGHT?

The fight-or-flight response (also called hyperarousal, or the acute stress response) is a physiological reaction that occurs in response to a perceived harmful event, attack, or threat to survival. It was first described by Walter Bradford Cannon. There are several different reactions we can take to impending disaster and I want to use this section to describe them in 'caricature', in relation to societal breakdown.

The Deniers

Unfortunately, denial seems to be on the increase. Many people just ignore all information that doesn't validate their existing 'filter bubble' ideology. Any information that challenges the mainstream narratives just gets labelled 'conspiracy theory' as in *'That's just a conspiracy theory isn't it?"* We seem to be so disconnected from ourselves, our nature and each other that we can simply believe whatever we want and justify its reality via whichever 'fake news' stream we choose to consume.

In perceiving the World, it is natural for us to edit, generalise and distort incoming information. We have to do this just to keep up with the 4,000 or so incoming messages inn a modern world. We need to label things just to make sense of the chaos that is happening around us. Many errors of perception occur as the flip side of this judgmental process.

Going by our record so far in trying to correct the errors of our ways, it seems we are happier as a species just monitoring our extinction rather than taking active steps to avoid it! Humans have an amazing capacity for believing what they choose and ignoring that which is painful. Because of this innate reality-editing faculty our society has become its own nemesis.

Errors of our perception may include:

- assuming other people hold the same views as us

- assuming people are consistent in their behaviour

- fixing our opinion of others to first or last impressions

- valuing some sorts of information above others

- having pre-formed attitudes

We often need to interpret 4,000 or so messages a day. Confronted with new information – we make judgements to make shortcuts and these 'errors of perception' often come into play. We do this in order to make sense of all the 'stuff' that just keeps coming. Reading statements like the ones below can be deeply scary:

- half of all wildlife lost in the last 40 years

- humans destroyed 10% of remaining wilderness in last 20 years

- global fisheries are collapsing

- Canadian wild salmon are radioactive

- insect populations are collapsing

- in the US – bees are on the endangered list

- coral reefs all over the planet are bleaching

- ice-melt is pouring into the sea

- a third of arable land has been lost in the last 30 years

- abrupt climate-change effects are imminent

- just 8 people own the same amount as wealth as half of the world's population

- half a billion people are obese

- nearly a billion people don't have enough to eat

- a billion children (half of the planet's population of children) live in poverty

- one in four people are mentally ill

- Trump got in

How do you deal with all this? The easiest response is just to deny it. There are different forms of denial that people use to prevent themselves from recognising the negative effects of our stories in the Western world, such as the Myth of Economic Growth. Some of these are:

- I don't think that these effects are really dangerous

- it just isn't my business to sort out these problems

- I pay my taxes so the government should sort it all out

- I don't want to be seen as a non-conformist

- this information is a threat to my interests

- this evidence is just being made up, I don't really believe it

- there's nothing we can do about it so I don't even want to talk about it

- that's just a conspiracy theory isn't it?

In this way, people manage to avoid facing our problems at all and they can get on with their lives.

Of course, once they do open Pandora's Box, it all gets pretty horrific and that's what frightens them. The second layer of denial, which I sometimes call 'We're Doomed Captain Mannering' (from a UK TV programme called Dads' Army) draws attention to the disasters increasingly created by the Myth of Economic Growth. It is an evidence based account, ignored by many, about the collapse of ecological and social systems, climate changes, the effect of the depletion of global and local resources such as those described in Transition's 'peak oil' and the sixth global mass extinction of species.

This is the standpoint of 'Woe is me', finger-wagging greenies who seem to want everyone to stop having fun and look after the planet because 'just look at what we are doing' – face of horror. Psychological barriers and responses that stop people entering into actually looking at the problems include:

- it's so upsetting I prefer not to think about it

- as soon as I start to think about the dangers I freeze up and feel panic. I feel paralysed

- there's no point in trying to do anything since it won't change a thing or make any difference

- we're doomed, give up

- we can fix it with new technology

- blitz consumerism – buy everything now

- human beings are a cancer on the earth and deserve to be wiped out anyway

- I expect Superman or God or aliens or Bill Gates or Richard Branson will save us all at the last minute

Once you can accept that climate change and species extinction are real, that the earth is badly polluted and in for a period of unpredictable change, you might be lucky enough to find 'Positive Hope' rather than 'Despair'. It is certainly one job of activists to help people overcome denial and accept a different reality. After all, its very hard to change anything when you can't accept what is happening. It seems to be a universally recognised position 'that in order to change something, you first have to accept it'. So the many deniers who would prefer to edit reality than face the problem are certainly part of the problem.

Many brave people are overcoming denial and are able to face the coming changes as already underway – as already past 'the tipping point'. Projects such as 'Dark Mountain', 'The Pachamama Alliance' or 'Ubuntu Planet' are inhabited by such people who are busy finding and making new myths and stories for a sad culture that seems committed to wrecking its own home.

It seems to be a universally recognised position 'that in order to change something, you first have to accept it'. So the many deniers who would prefer to edit reality than face the problem are certainly part of the problem.

The Survivalists

Get off-grid, learn about hunting, foraging and making stuff with your hands. Stock up on tinned and dried food and bury it all in an underground bunker in the middle of nowhere. Buy guns and ammo. Get ready to shoot people and eat them.

Also known as 'Preppers' in the states, some of the low-tech, 'redneck' solutions these people provide for eg, solar showers, free hot baths, rocket stoves, underground shelters or greenhouses, natural swimming pools, eco-cooking are nothing short of brilliant. Resilience is an important part of an unstable future and if for example, all the supermarkets and shops were empty, for whatever reason' how long could you survive? If your power went off for a week, or a month – what would you do. It is essential to consider these things and have a plan in any case.

The Moralists

When you look around, the 'green' choice sometimes seems just another colour of consumer capitalism. Often it is the more expensive option in a choice to buy goods. Being a 'green consumer' is rife with hypocrisies and although it might make for a good conscience it is still little more than a fashion statement. Somewhere along the line corporate consumerism has already hi-jacked many of the real intentions beyond being 'green'.

Surely recycle, reduce, repair and re-use and refuse are the essence of the green message? As opposed to 'purchase from a different source'.

Certainly there seem to be better consumer options available with green shopping, such as buying 'Fair Trade'. But there are many people who now question just how fair any trade with third world countries can be in the context of the international banking and free trade system we have. It can't be right to buy something cheap from a Third World country and then sell it expensive to the First World customers?

In reality to be 'green', one should let go of all attachment to money and close one's bank account. In reality the green option here is local trade and exchange with local produce and without the use of money. Even the most ethical of banks is still part of an earth-wrecking system that exploits the non-renewable raw materials of the earth. This economic system is built on the fallacy that we can continue to use our capital assets, the resources of the Earth, as income in a 'growth forever' fantasy.

In reality, being green means letting go of your job and refusing to use petrol to go to work at all. Almost all employment is also part of the same economic system that exploits people and planet for the profit of a few, and the payment for this employment is money – which is at the heart of our problem in creating a fairer social system.

In reality, being green means not buying anything at all. It means making, growing, mending or exchanging goods and avoiding money which is taxed by governments to further their warmongering economic objectives and the objectives of their controllers, with its unavoidable side effects of environmental and planetary degradation.

In reality, being green means turning off your gas, your electricity and your water supply because the systems that deliver these to you are also entrenched in the earth destroying, monopolist systems of consumer capitalism.

Anything less is a compromise. But whose going to do that (apart from Mark Boyle)?

Promoting, even suggesting such options in today's world is often met with stony silence. In a world controlled by fear of terrorism, any kind of extremism or radicalism is increasingly interpreted as dangerous and anti-social, a threat to the system or part of a 'conspiracy' based reaction. How long do you think government will take to accuse 'Extinction Rebellion' of economic terrorism?

There aren't many people who are actually able to be truly 'green'. Often those whose cultures are naturally sustainable in resource terms, like the Kalahari Bushmen or the Masai, like the indigenous peoples of the Amazon Basin, Australia or North America, are persecuted and forced into unsustainable systems in which they have to earn money to provide for themselves and their families.

So a moralist will refuse to earn enough money to pay taxes. They are unlikely to have a car or a house. They may not vote or buy stuff and stay out of consumerist cycles by not owning. They re-use and recycle as much as possible and avoid contributing any of their valuable energy to the system. Food is sourced on an ethical basis and possibly purchased by direct exchange if possible. A moralist activist might opt-out to a co-operative lifestyle, living off the land in domes, benders or mini-homes and getting by on part-time jobs.

Of course one solution is to change culture and move somewhere beautiful like Northern Thailand where people still live a spiritual life in tune with nature. As write this in January in the Northern hemisphere, two days after Trump's inauguration, this seems a particularly tempting opt-out at the moment.

The Activists

"Subversion, resistance and epic spanner-chucking are an integral part of a sane response to world death. The global resistance movement has neither the time or the power to dismantle the ruinous market system before nature has her say."

Lierre Keith – Deep Green Resistance

Your mission, should you choose to accept it, is to persuade people that when laws are made to be unjust, civil disobedience is not only justified, it is essential. Techniques of resistance, protest and 'spanner chucking' are essential (more on this later). Resisting the dominant hegemony, challenging it at every turn and revealing truths are important actions to change to change the dominant stories. Extrapolating our often unquestioned human actions and 'bad stories' to their resultant conclusions helps people to think about the consequences of their actions.

Every act of progression in a nation's history has involved tension with law, whether it was the formation of parliament itself, the abolition of slavery, the enfranchisement of women or the 'birth of a nation' enshrined in a constitution. Laws had to be broken because they were wrong and they prevented the situation from changing. Remember, apartheid was legal, the Holocaust was legal, Colonialism was legal. Legality is a matter of power, not justice.

Perhaps you still believe, like many people, that our existing government systems can be reformed in time to make a difference? Perhaps your activism is still invested in a vote?

The Terrorists

I fully realise that if I advocate terrorism in what is a public document that I am liable to be arrested under current laws. So I am stating quite clearly here that I am **not doing this**. But where civil disobedience ends and terrorism begins is an important discussion, especially in the face of completely unjust legislation. It's a fine line and even advocating what might be 'perceived as terrorism' on social media can get you arrested in this age of enforced paranoia. As I am writing this my Facebook media stream tells me that Madonna is presently under investigation by the Secret Service for publicly admitting that she had 'thought about blowing up the Whitehouse'. Now that's a pop video I would pay to see!

With the advent of the US 'Ministry of Truth' – it seems that thought crime, (or at least 'admitting to thought' crime until they can snoop our minds,) is already a reality in the US. When combined with the UK's 'Investigatory Powers Act' – its easy to see how we now have legislation that can easily discover what anyone with a phone or computer is thinking.

I write novels (as well as books like this one) and I have been researching a Royalist pamphleteer called Silas Titus who was considering the assassination of Cromwell in 1663. He persuaded himself that such an assassination would be just killing rather than murder because it would be 'tyrannicide' – the killing of a tyrant.

In a similar way, some of the more extreme 'green terrorists' would advocate the destruction of property and people to promote their cause. The logic is if you can kill a few now to make people aware enough to act and save millions – then this act of terrorism is actually saving people. Bond villians are made of such! Weird logic I know – but where is the line when we have such oppressive laws being enforced?

Spoiling your vote is OK, in fact Caroline Lucas advocates in her book that this is a better choice than not voting, as not voting smacks of lethargy. But ballot box bombs – incendiary devices that destroy all the votes in the box? Definitely terrorism. In this material world the line seems to be that terrorism involves the destruction of property, places or people. Ironic indeed when these are the very outcomes of capitalism in action.

Positive Hope

"Materialism feeds and empowers the ego-mind. The ego is the overshadowing psychic force driving the self-perpetuating illusion of materialistic self-image. It's the voice that tells you that you are what you label yourself to be; that you are your thoughts; that you are something to be defined. When in truth, nothing is definable. We are all simply an amalgamation of quantum energy — part of an incomprehensible process of energy and frequency convergence within a vast cosmological continuum of expansion and contraction."

Finding positive hope means experiencing transformation at a personal level. It involves the use of creative energy to change the poisons of the toxic myth of Economic Growth into the nectar of a life sustaining society committed to the healing and recovery of our world.

It can be deeply challenging and exciting. It means being closely in touch with your values and choosing to live an ethical life filled with personally generated meaning. It means existing in a state of compassion and love as much as you can. It means being dedicated to personal excellence rather than 'competitiveness'. There are more and more people looking for and finding this.

The New Sciences tells us that we are all made of energy. We are here to enjoy the experience of being alive. We are here to make things better for each other because if you suffer – I suffer. I admit I am sometimes racked with fury and sadness at what I see people are doing to this beautiful planet, often without even noticing. In reality I swing between finding beauty and solace in the place and moment and despair for what a culture of ignorant idiots are doing to my world.

I live in a very pleasant place, the least inhabited area of Cornwall UK, where the summer lanes are alive with wildflowers and all sorts of wildlife. When I see people driving their cars through these lanes and just chucking their rubbish out of the windows – I find it hard to believe that I am the same species as these wreckers.

I attempt to live in a relationship with the nature around me, sharing a yield from my garden with nature, living lightly on the earth. The farmer on the dairy farm next to us likes to shoot the rooks out of our trees because they 'make a noise', whilst filling the valley with his own noise pollution from his farm vehicles. This feeling of being an alien on my own planet perseveres.

My brothers and sisters, the indigenous peoples of this earth such as the Kogi, the Kayapo, Lakota and Sioux Indians, Masai or Australian Aboriginals live in tune with the earth around them, as much as they can. They have different stories to our own, ones that don't end with the destruction of our environment. But our stories of economic growth also despoil these peoples – we are taking them over the edge with us! We are systematically destroying the very peoples who can help us!

James Lovelock explains a sense of linked awareness in his Gaia Hypothesis:

"The Gaia hypothesis, also known as Gaia theory, proposes that organisms interact with their inorganic surroundings on Earth to form a self-regulating, complex system that contributes to maintaining the conditions for life on the planet. Topics of interest include how the biosphere and the evolution of life forms affect the stability of global temperature, ocean salinity, oxygen in the atmosphere and other environmental variables that affect the habitability of Earth."

Wikipedia

The Gaia Hypothesis is at least an entry level into eco-theology in the First World. It attributes complexity and interactiveness to our planet – with the people who inhabit it as part of that system.

The present mass extinction event, named 'The Holocene Extinction', is also mainly due to activity from earth's inhabitants – in this case, humans and their industrial excrements. A great cycle of life described by David Attenborough as 'abundance, destruction, rebirth' is reaching the end of its second phase for humans, sometimes called the Sixth Extinction. It appears that the occasional desolation of the planet by its occupants may be part of an ongoing evolutionary process.

At a personal level, in order to transcend my sadness about what people are doing to my planet, one of the things I have recently taken to telling myself that 'Everything is as it should be'. Perhaps this too is a form of denial? As long as I make my own personal choices to 'do no harm', to live on this planet lightly, without unnecessarily destroying life or damaging eco-systems, I cannot accept responsibility for all the

114

dumbed-down idiots out there who choose not to look at the consequences of their actions.

But what if all of the species of this earth, including 'Industrial Age Humans', are unknowingly part of a mass, 'Gaian' consciousness. Then perhaps our fatal human flaw – denial – is an important element in the overall evolution of life?

Perhaps the fatal flaw at the heart of Holocene people, human nature itself, is there for a reason. Maybe humans are somehow programmed to alter the environment of their own planet in the service of the evolution of life? Perhaps we need this pressure on to make the changes?

One role as an activist is to try and bring a sense of the spiritual to mundane everday existence and I feel very lucky in being able to do so – to experience the moments of peak connection with life around me. I believe one of the problems with the 'wetiko' materialists is that they lack any sense of connection because they have never had an authentic spiritual experience that connects them with the 'whole'. As a result their drive is to accumulate far more than they need is to fill up the empty space of disconnection. To ameliorate their insecurity through possession.

Seyyed Hossein Nasr, a prominent Islamic philosopher, identifies:

"The ecological crisis is only an externalization of an inner malaise and it cannot be solved without a spiritual rebirth…"

The undervaluing of creativity in our culture, along with independence of thought and imagination is preventing our species from evolving its narrative and myth making faculties enough to realise the changes we need. 'Wetiko thinking' tells us that we can't affect reality with our thoughts, imagination or visionary capacities. It's dependence on keeping the lie going stops us from creating the new stories we desperately need in these times.

6. SHIFTING DEMOCRACY

Can Government be Changed?

'If life on earth is to continue, the global political and economic structures need to be dismantled and the local structures need to engage with their communities.'

An analysis by mathematicians shows that human society has become too complex for representative democracy to work. Jason Koebler, in an online article 'Society Is Too Complicated to Have a President' writes:

"It is absurd, then, to believe that the concentration of power in one or a few individuals at the top of a hierarchical representative democracy will be able to make optimal decisions on a vast array of connected and complex issues that will certainly have sweeping and unintended ramifications on other parts of human civilization."

He quotes Yaneer Bar-Yam, the New England Complex Systems Institutes (NECSI)'s director:

"There's a natural process of increasing complexity in the world and we can recognize that at some point, that increase in complexity is going to run into the complexity of the individual. And at that point, hierarchical organizations will fail. We were raised to believe that democracy, and even the democracy that we have, is a system that has somehow inherent good to it. Hierarchical organizations are failing in the response to decision-making challenges. And this is true whether we're talking about dictatorships, or communism that had very centralized control processes, and for representative democracies today. Representative democracies still focus power in one or few individuals. And that concentration of control and decision-making makes those systems ineffective.

During the time of ancient empires, large-scale human systems executed relatively simple behaviors, and individuals performed relatively simple individual tasks that were repeated by many individuals over time to have a large scale effect.

We cannot expect one individual to know how to respond to the challenges of the world today. So whether we talk about one candidate or another, the Democrats or Republicans, Clinton versus Trump. The real question ultimately is, will we be able to change the system?

We've become fundamentally confused about what the decisions are, and what their consequences are. And we can't make a connection between them. And that's true about everybody, as well as about the decision-makers, the policymaker. They don't know what the effects will be of the decisions that they're making.

We end up with people who will say, 'I will do this, and things will be better.' And another person who will say, 'I will do this. And things will do better.' And we can't tell. Right now the danger is that we will choose strategies that will really cause a lot of destruction, before we've created the ability to make better decisions."

Original article at: https://motherboard.vice.com/en_us/article/society-is-too-complicated-to-have-a-president-complex-mathematics-suggest

The notion of sovereignty developed from the idea that people were stronger in groups. They would appoint a 'leader', who would often give fealty to a group leader, such as a regional King or Monarch. Later this sovereignty became invested in the Senate or Parliament where it now resides.

From the UK government website comes:

"In the UK dissolution is the official term for the end of a Parliament. Under the Fixed-term Parliaments Act 2011 a general election must be held in the UK, and a new Parliament elected, every five years. Under the Fixed-term Parliaments Act 2011 a Parliament is dissolved 25 working days before the general election. Parliament was last dissolved on 30 March 2015.

Parliament may be 'prorogued' a few days before being dissolved. At prorogation all parliamentary business ends, although that Parliament would still exist until dissolution. The 2014-15 session of Parliament was prorogued on Thursday 26 March 2015.

When Parliament has been dissolved the Monarch issues a royal proclamation summoning the new Parliament. The royal proclamation is published in the London and Edinburgh Gazettes. The Prime Minister asked Her Majesty to summon the new Parliament to meet on Monday 18 May 2015, when the business was the election of the Commons Speaker and the swearing-in of members. The State Opening of Parliament took place on Wednesday 27 May 2015.

When Parliament is dissolved, every seat in the House of Commons becomes vacant. All business in the House comes to an end. There are no Members of Parliament. MPs revert to being members of the public and lose privileges associated with being a Member of Parliament.

MPs are allowed access to Parliament for just a few days in which to remove papers from their offices. The facilities that the House provides for MPs in Westminster during a Parliament are no longer available to them from 5pm on the day of dissolution. Until a new Parliament is elected, there are no MPs. Those who wish to be MPs again must stand again as candidates for election. The Speaker is no longer an MP once Parliament is dissolved as there are no longer any MPs until the new Parliament is returned. Like every other MP, the Speaker must stand for re-election at a general election if he or she wishes to become an MP again. If the Speaker stands as a candidate in the election they stand as 'Speaker seeking re-election'.

Members of the House of Lords are appointed, not elected. Members of the House of Lords retain their positions, but all business in the House comes to an end when Parliament is dissolved. While Members of the Lords can access the premises of Parliament, only limited facilities and services are available to them.

It is customary for the Prime Minister to recommend new life peerages for some former MPs to the Queen at the end of a Parliament in a Dissolution Honours list.

The Government does not resign when Parliament is dissolved. Government ministers remain in charge of their departments until after the result of the election is known and a new administration is formed.

The Prime Minister is appointed by the Sovereign. Ministers are appointed by the Sovereign on the advice of the Prime Minister. These appointments are independent of the role of MP. Ministers retain their ministerial titles after dissolution, but those who were MPs can no longer use the MP suffix.

The Cabinet Manual sets out the main laws, rules and conventions affecting the conduct and operation of government."

http://www.parliament.uk/about/how/elections-and-voting/general/dissolution/

Dissolution of UK Parliament

There seem to be only two ways that Parliament can be constitutionally dissolved. One method would be via a registered political party, such as 'Vox Pop' whose sole reason for existence would be to reform Parliament from the inside. It seeks to change the face of Parliament completely from the (alleged) representative democracy we have to one in which people manage themselves, like a participatory democracy.

So there is really no mechanism within Parliament beyond this for it to evolve to a form of democracy more suitable to the 21st Century. Given that even the much fairer representative system of 'proportional representation' has never been adopted, due to the vested interest of the larger political parties, the likelihood of such a change happening is marginal at best. Although communications technology has advanced exponentially in the 21st Century the processes of Parliament seem to remain in the 18th Century.

It may be possible for people in the UK to lobby the ruling monarch to ask them to 'refuse to summon the new Parliament' because they no longer operate in the interests of society and individuals, but that of corporate power. I suspect that this is a standpoint that might find sympathy with some members of our Royal Family. Instead of the present setup, we might move to a system of voting where every person was able to vote on every issue, which I have called 'participatory democracy'. The government would then, once again become the servants of the people where they are meant to be.

Legally Dissolving American Government

According to an online article by Skip Sanders there is a mechanism by which the U.S. Federal Government can be legally dissolved.

"Thirty four (34) is the number of Legislatures from the several States necessary to call a States Convention or a Constitutional Convention. This also known as an Article Five (5) Convention, or a Convention to Amend the U.S. Constitution. With fifty (50) States in the U.S. Federal Compact today, thirty four (34) is the Constitutional number of legislatures from the several States needed to cross the threshold for such a convention.

Let's look at Article 5 of the U.S. Constitution :

"The Congress, whenever two thirds of both Houses shall deem it necessary, shall propose Amendments to this Constitution, or, on the Application of the Legislatures of two thirds of the several States, shall call a Convention for proposing Amendments, which, in either Case, shall be valid to all Intents and Purposes, as Part of this Constitution, when ratified by the Legislatures of three fourths of the several States or by Conventions in three fourths thereof, as the one or the other Mode of Ratification may be proposed by the Congress; Provided that no Amendment which may be made prior to the Year One thousand eight hundred and eight shall in any Manner affect the first and fourth Clauses in the Ninth Section of the first Article; and that no State, without its Consent, shall be deprived of its equal Suffrage in the Senate."

Thirty eight (38) is the number of legislatures from the several States that is necessary to ratify and thus amend the U.S. Constitution after such a convention. This amendment could be 'to dissolve'. By 'dissolve' I mean the whole compact between the several States. Yes, the entire Federal Government and every thing it has or was created under it's jurisdiction. This would include but is not limited too, the Federal Debt, the Federal Reserve Bank, the FDIC, the Department of Education, the Department of Homeland Security, the Army, the Navy, the Air Force, the Marines, etc. etc... Think of it as a Constitutional self destruct mechanism.

This would leave the fifty (50) several States and the numerous Federal Territories, sovereign and under their own rightful and direct jurisdiction. Of course each State or Territory would then be free to individually or in groups engage in new compacts and trade arrangements. That is up to them to decide at a further date.

I know this information is very powerful and the far reaching ramification of such a decision may be a little hard for the reader to grasp or understand at first glance. I openly admit that I am not capable of understanding all the possibilities or consequences of such a decision. That being said, please allow me to entertain some ideas that immediately come to mind.

The Federal Reserve and Federal Reserve Notes are gone. The National Debt under the Federal Governments' promise to pay, evaporates Of course the IRS and all Federal Taxes. Social Security, Medicare and all that has been promised, owed or collected. Any claim to Federal Park Lands, highways, military bases, equipment, buildings, assets of any kind inside the several States. Any and all Federal agreements or treaties such as NATO, the UN, WTO, NAFTA,CAFTA, GAT and so on. I invite the readers to speculate and comment on any of the challenges or possibilities that could result if such a course was taken.

I will leave you with this final thought, *"That which has been created can NOT be greater than the creator."* It is time for the people through their several State Governments assert their power over the Federal Government over which they created. 100% Legally with pen and paper!"

Although it may be technically possible to dissolve governments legally, it is pretty impossible given the urgent time frame. What could replace them?

Random Democracy

I include a process of democracy here called 'Sortition' as it illuminates one of the present problems with our current leaders in Parliament and Senate. They do not represent our interest and are one the whole, out of touch with ordinary people. It costs a lot of money and time to get elected so it is no wonder that nearly all candidates are representing the interests of money and economics. We have a fiscal oligarchy not a democracy. With Sortition this problem is neatly sidestepped. It is my belief that even a *random lottery to fill parliament* would serve the people of the UK and US better than the bunch of pirates presently in control. From Wikipedia:

"Athenian democracy developed in the 6th century BC out of what was then called isonomia (equality of law and political rights). Sortition was then the principal way of achieving this fairness. It was utilized to pick most of the magistrates for their governing committees, and for their juries (typically of 501 men). Aristotle relates equality and democracy:

"Democracy arose from the idea that those who are equal in any respect are equal absolutely. All are alike free, therefore they claim that all are free absolutely... The next is when the democrats, on the grounds that they are all equal, claim equal participation in everything".

It is accepted as democratic when public offices are allocated by lot; and as oligarchic when they are filled by election. In Athens, 'democracy' (literally meaning rule by the people) was in opposition to those supporting a system of oligarchy (rule by a few). Athenian democracy was characterised by being run by the 'many' (the ordinary people) who were allotted to the committees which ran government. The Athenians believed sortition to be more democratic than elections and used complex procedures with purpose-built allotment machines (kleroteria) to avoid the corrupt practices used by oligarchs to buy their way into office.

According to the author Mogens Herman Hansen the citizen's court was superior to the assembly because the allotted members swore an oath which ordinary citizens in the assembly did not and therefore the court could annul the decisions of the assembly. Both Aristotle and Herodotus (one of the earliest writers on democracy) emphasize selection by lot as a test of democracy,

"The rule of the people has the fairest name of all, equality (isonomia), and does none of the things that a monarch does. The lot determines offices, power is held accountable, and deliberation is conducted in public."

Past scholarship maintained that sortition had roots in the use of chance to divine the will of the gods, but this view is no longer common among scholars. In Ancient Greek mythology, Zeus, Poseidon, and Hades used sortition to determine who ruled over which domain. Zeus got the sky, Poseidon the sea, and Hades the underworld.

In Athens, to be eligible to be chosen by lot, citizens self-selected themselves into the available pool, then lotteries in the kleroteria machines. The magistracies assigned by lot generally had terms of service of 1 year. A citizen could not hold magistracy more than once in his lifetime, but could hold other magistracies. All male citizens over 30 years of age, who were not disenfranchised by atimia, were eligible. Those selected through lot underwent examination called dokimasia in order to avoid incompetent officials. Rarely were selected citizens discarded. Magistrates, once in place, were subjected to constant monitoring by the Assembly. Magistrates appointed by lot had to render account of their time in office upon their leave, called euthynai. However, any citizen could request the suspension of a magistrate with due reason".

https://en.wikipedia.org/wiki/Sortition

The process of sortition may be more than just an ancient Athenian dream. One of the conditions asked for by the activist group Extinction Rebellion includes "By necessity these demands require initiatives and mobilisation of similar size and scope to those enacted in times of war. We do not however, trust our Government to make the bold, swift and long-term changes necessary to achieve this and we do not intend to hand further power to our politicians. Instead we demand a Citizens' Assembly to oversee the changes, as we rise from the wreckage, creating a democracy fit for purpose."

It is being discussed that a process of sortition may offer more headway in this process than our impossibly-slow-to-act systems of government.

Participatory Democracy

"Are we building in service of the people and the community, deeply rooted in social values and human rights, or are we in service of private interests, which only answer to their own internal logic of profit and power?"

singularityhub.com

One of the protections against government corruption in democracies is that the moment of our vote is hidden and blind, made in secret in a kiosk. When an individual can use new governance technologies to summon a dashboard of her votes, might that make her more vulnerable to coercion from people who can verify whether or not she is voting the way that they want? Is anybody thinking carefully about how to get around this issue?

In our current political system, it makes sense that hidden votes are so important. But the very idea that our key moment of agency as a citizen is ticking a box every few years is the insane part. Just putting the act of voting online doesn't actually change anything about the underlying dynamic, and I think it's a red herring.

Instead of talking about how we're going to prevent corruption in the digital equivalent of the same old system, can we talk about the transformative power of deliberative democracy? What's actually incredible is when you create a society where people not only feel safe being open about their political opinions, but they genuinely discuss them with different people, and their opinion can evolve through that interaction — they can change their minds. When citizen deliberation is possible, that's when truly amazing solutions can emerge, from synthesizing different views.

Let's talk about direct citizen engagement, instead of electing some person that got on the ballot through a broken, convoluted process in the first place, to play a crazy politics game that has almost nothing to do with representing you, the box ticker. Our 'democratic' system is another example of something developed a couple hundred years ago because of very limited communications technology — election dates in the US are still determined by how long it took people to go on horseback between cities. We can do so much better."

https://singularityhub.com/2015/12/18/stay-tuned-for-the-technological-transformation-of-government/

In an Age of Communication we no longer need a Parliamentary Democracy. The voting system and the whole idea of a 'representative democracy by proxy' is an anachronism. We no longer need an archaic system by which potential politicians have to tell us what we want to hear, in order to become our chosen representatives, to pursue their own agendas in an inept and corrupt government system.

Successive governments whether of the left or of the right have already sold our sovereignty to the highest bidder, big business. They are supported in this by the mega-corporation owned media, education systems, health services, big energy and other industry biased services and socioeconomic structures. They exist to serve an 'economy' that is destroying the optimum conditions for life on earth. Our support of this economy is at the cost of our ecology, the integrity of nature we need to live.

The 'business interest' domination of our lives is enforced by the police, and increasingly hired security thugs, who are technically here to serve us, the people. Government acts in the interest of big business and the economy, which has become entirely contrary to the interests of sustainable and healthy life on this planet.

Already, organisations such as change.org are stepping into the breach to engage more with people as a neccessary aid to a failing democracy.

"As citizens, we shape our democracies by not being silent. A healthy, vibrant democracy flourishes when people have an opportunity to debate the issues that matter to them, when our efforts to create change pay off, and our voices are heard. Only then, can we end the kind of discontent and anger driving our politics.

With our daily work at Change.org, we help strengthen our democracy by giving everyday people an opportunity to shape the world around them. We are fiercely independent and non-partisan because every person in the world having a voice is bigger than party politics. No one deserves to be powerless.

This has never been more urgent. Regardless of your political perspective it's clear that across the world divisiveness, fear, and terror play an increasing part in our lives. People feel ignored by elites and a political class that's out of touch.

We need to build a political system where people can more easily participate, engage with elected representatives and ultimately understand each other better. Through supporting everyday people to connect and speak up, we'll bring about positive change. And we'll hold the powerful accountable – whoever they may be: the politicians, corporate and cultural leaders that represent us.

Change.org's mission is to create a world where no one is powerless. We're just getting started, by providing a free, open, empowering platform that helps people unite on the issues they care about to create change, amplify people's stories and transform lives."

change.org

If you look at other online lobbying bodies such as 38degrees.org.uk, causes.com, or ipetitions.com you can see a system developing by which people can express their choices to government. At present in the UK, if a petition gets 100,000 signatures it will be considered for debate in Parliament.

It doesn't take a genius to connect 'referendums and online petitions' to create a system by which people can govern themselves by direct voting. In fact you can see how this might work here: http://voxpopgov.com/ and an online 'place' for this already exists in the UK at www.gov.uk.

The Brexit Referendum

Since the Brexit referendum is an example of direct participatory democracy in action, its worth investigating. Yvette Cooper analyses how we voted in Brexit:

"The cities voted in. Industrial towns voted out. Digital growth areas like the M4 corridor or the University towns voted in. The Tory shires and the Labour coalfields voted out. Scotland voted in. England and Wales voted out. The young voted in. Older votes chose out. Graduates in. Working-class communities out.

Those who saw globalisation as an opportunity voted in. Those who felt globalisation was a threat and didn't trust 'the system' to make it better voted out ... Communities who didn't believe the Remain Campaign's arguments about risk because they didn't feel they had much more to lose. People who said they didn't believe experts, because too often experts have let them down ...

A Tory prime minister could not persuade them. Because a Tory government has let them down. But Labour had nothing to say that could convince them either. They weren't convinced by staying in Europe because they couldn't see how they benefited.

We are here without a plan because politics has failed. Because our political process just couldn't deal with the difficult issues so they got worse. Because too many of our politicians couldn't work out how to solve problems so they made false promise or just walked away. Because too many towns feel they have no future. Because immigration seemed too hard to solve. Because the EU seemed too hard to reform. Because inequality is still rising and it seemed too hard to stop. Because we weren't prepared to take action to sort out housing. Because trust collapsed. And with every layer of failure, politics just made it worse."

The Brexit referendum in the UK is itself an example of participatory democracy. In spite of its false dichotomy, to be either 'in or out' of Europe, 72% of us voted directly on an issue. The outcome proved that the Parliamentary system of representation is not working – it is not even remotely in touch with the people. It was a result they didn't expect that resulted in the prime minister resigning.

According to the Brexit referendum vote we were either 'in or out' of the European Union. The reality, even with a 'hard Brexit' will be years of negotiation that defines our relationship with Europe, clearly not black or white but many shades. Similarly our government of whatever shade is presented as either left or right – we are seriously limiting our options as to what is possible by voting for a government who only exist in black and white.

The Brexit vote that surprised everybody is little more than a plea to end the interminable intervention of intrusive government in every aspect of our lives, telling us what we can and can't do, can and can't eat, where we can and can't go, what we should and shouldn't think. It is a call for the end of being ineptly governed by people who are wholly out of touch with their electorate. It's beyond time to get rid of politicians entirely, they are only getting worse!

From an article, *'We Need a Revolution'* by Martin Winiecki

"In the United States, the anger and hatred that has long been boiling in millions of people has now found its political outlet. Trump's success has been unprecedented and overwhelming. His simple message resonates in large parts of the American society, in people who have long felt betrayed, abused and disenfranchised by an alienated 'establishment.' Trump wins against all reasoning of decency because he recklessly breaks what his supporters most despise: 'political correctness.' He understands how to play the emotional piano of the masses; he's the ultimate caricature of a society teeming with universal corruption and sexual perversion.

The rise of fascism always seems to hit the world by surprise. Yet what we are now witnessing has not begun with Trump, just as German fascism had not begun with Hitler. Wherever people are prohibited to express their basic emotional and energetic drives, wherever they grow up and live in conditions of fear, mistrust and violence, the danger of fascism looms. Suppressed life energy dams up and turns into constant aggression. When the container of the bourgeois order crumbles, when people lose their jobs, voices and prospects – as it has gradually happened in this era of expanding corporate dominance – and the state no longer succeeds in controlling violence, the monstrous force of bottled-up emotions breaks free. Once they have a strong paternal authority telling them whom to blame, declaring them to be a collective that will now exact revenge, people get together in wild exaltation. Finally they have a channel and they develop a threatening force.

We must not despise or ridicule these people, but understand how they have gotten into the desperate state they are in. Thereby fascism is no longer a thing of 'the others'; it's something that concerns us all. The psychoanalyst Dieter Duhm writes,

"Latent fascism is present everywhere; it is the cancer of humanity… It develops in the subconscious of our human relationships. In the emotional substrata of a misguided civilization lie the horrible powers that led to Nazi Germany and which currently lead to very similar atrocities in many countries on Earth."

People call for boycotting companies who employ refugees from Muslim countries and threaten the people running them. Attacks on people of color, other religions and political ideologies have steeply increased. People no longer see any prospect for the future. They no longer have anything in this world they can believe in. Unable of loving, retaliation is what gives them strength. Similar explosions of hatred are occurring all over the world. When we witness what political prisoners in Turkey (neglected by our Western leaders) or the civilians trapped inside the besieged cities of Aleppo and Mosul are now facing, we know that this global culture has come to a turning point.

Yet the aggression now explicitly exploding among white lower-class Americans is only a miniature version of the ruthless warfare systematically orchestrated by this country's elites for many decades. War is an essential component of our entire economic system – one without which this system would instantaneously collapse. While 'decent' Americans show themselves outraged about Trump, their candidate for President has her blueprints ready for expanding military interventionism around the world. Democratic Ex-President Obama has already bombed seven Islamic countries and ordered the drone assassination of thousands of innocent children and women abroad, but he is considered 'moderate' in terms of warfare compared to Hillary Clinton. In the current escalation with Russia and China there no longer seems to be any limit. We mustn't be surprised by what is now erupting inside America. Similar to how it was in the late Roman Empire, the American Empire is entering a phase of self-destruction as it is being eaten up by the very violence it has used to establish itself in the first place. And with it goes the entire capitalist world order this country has essentially shaped.

Trump is nothing other than a mirror for the world to look into, a call to awaken before it's too late. It is silly to blame the mirror for what you see in it. Trump is not the enemy; he is merely the symptom of a culture worshipping power, violence and greed. If you are afraid of Trump, what you are actually afraid of is this culture and its socio-economic system. Stopping fascism isn't achieved through ideological battles; it is rather a matter of building a new and humane culture. This is nothing short of a global revolution. A revolution from bottom up, on all levels of society.

We need a revolution that establishes new foundations for human life on Earth, new foundations for our coexistence with each other and nature. A revolution that allows us to remember the sacredness of life and of all living beings. We need a revolution for solidarity and trust; *"a revolution,"* as Dieter Duhm says, *"whose victory will create no losers because it will achieve a state that benefits all."*

...This new revolution will not be achieved by shifting political power from one party to another, but by establishing forms of coexistence which allow the human being to liberate himself from all disguises and reconnect in trust. Every fascist will transform into a loving person, every terrorist into a caretaker for life, if he or she can find home in a community that allows closed hearts to open again. This is not a matter of therapy, but of the social, sexual, ethical and economic structures we live in. Building a movement based on communities of trust would not only be a genuine alternative to the fascist threat emerging everywhere; it may also set the foundations for the new global culture we as humanity need in order to have a future worth living on this planet."

"I have come to understand that we first of all need something like a revolution of consciousness and a profound transformation of our social systems if we want to avert short-term regression into the primitive authoritarianism with which we are now threatened, as well as long-term ecological meltdown. I agree with him that this revolution is not simply a matter of changing our political or economic system; the solution has to be primarily spiritual and secondarily political."

Russell Brand

Anarchy is preferable

"We are in a race against time – against mass species extinction, increasing inequality, ecological collapse, etc. – and every day that we do not try to affect change at the structural level is a day lost."

As I explained in the preface, anarchy is not the same as chaos. Here, once more is the definition with which I am working in this book:

"a theory holding all forms of governmental authority to be unnecessary and undesirable and advocating a society based on voluntary co-operation and free association of individuals and groups."

What is needed is a new socio-economic model that is within the carrying capacity of Planet Earth. For this people need to accept that responsibility and freedom are intimately intertwined.

"People go on talking about freedom but they don't want freedom exactly, they want irresponsibility. They ask for freedom, but deep down, unconsciously, they ask for irresponsibility; license. Freedom is maturity; license is very childish. Freedom is possible only when you are so integrated that you can take the responsibility of being free...A healthy person is always aware that whatever they are doing, they are responsible. The very idea of responsibility will give you a freedom, a dignity." Osho

I will leave it to 'The Anarchist Studies Network' to explain below where an anarchist standpoint fits into the shift from a parliamentary, representative democracy to a directly participatory democracy.

Present government... "is looking to roll back the state. Anarchists want this too, but the government is looking to roll back the state and let business take up the slack, thereby bringing a fictitious 'free market' into every last recess of our lives. That's where the disagreement lies. Anarchists advocate practical alternatives to both this neoliberal slash-and-burn policy and the old Labour state-socialism...

Anarchists do not believe that state socialism is the only alternative to the undemocratic inequalities produced by neoliberalism. Socialising property does not have to mean nationalising it – that would simply be substituting one set of bosses for another. What about genuine collective worker ownership of industry and services; what about universities democratically run by academics, students and support staff, instead of largely unaccountable and overpaid managers and technocrats?

More widely, couldn't we radicalise the co-operative model and have all companies democratically owned and run by their managers and workers? Couldn't we expand and federate worker co-ops, mutuals and collectives? The movement for fan-ownership of football clubs is a further indication that these kinds of alternatives work. The challenge is to think through their potential, and anarchism provides such a framework.

Because this fake democracy doesn't work and the interests of anarchists could never be represented by a political party, direct action is the tactic of choice. And direct action is part of the process of creating direct democracy. It produces results by raising the profile of causes and often halting practices many object to.

As well as a tactic, direct action is also a means for self-empowerment. It is a component of the society we hope to create, where people take control of their lives into their own hands and confront the root causes of injustices directly, without representatives. This sometimes includes property damage, but anarchists take seriously the notions of liberty and equality: that people are capable of speaking and acting for themselves and become even more capable through practice rather than representation.

The threat to a liveable world comes not from anarchists or terrorists, but from governments and capitalism. Before the current crisis is used as a front to take us even deeper into a neoliberal nightmare, let's reconsider alternatives."

The Anarchist Studies Network is a specialist group of the UK Political Studies Association. This piece was collectively written but does not necessarily reflect a consensus view.

Phase Transition

From Jeremy Lent: "In the very darkness of the times ahead, there is reason for hope that this bleak period will be the harbinger of a transformed society: a new economic and social order based on principles of equity, compassion, and natural flourishing.

The source of this hope emerges from research in complex systems – and more specifically, how phase transitions occur in these systems.

While a complex system can remain resilient within a set of parameters for a long time, occasionally it becomes so unstable that it experiences a tipping point: a dramatic shift that transforms the system into something very different.

As we look at the current political situation, many signs suggest that we're arriving at a new, historic tipping point. The globally dominant neoliberal political-economic system has caused unprecedented wealth and income inequalities, which have destabilized the foundations on which the past seventy years of relative peace and prosperity have been built. The Brexit shock, the rise of neo-fascism in Europe, and the impending cataclysm of Trump's lawless brutality seem to signal an approaching tipping point. Our global society is most likely about to enter a phase transition, after which it will emerge into a new, stable state.

During a phase transition, a system goes through a chaotic period of shifting power dynamics. In this period, seemingly insignificant actions can have an outsize effect, sometimes dramatically impacting the character of the long-term outcome. When we apply this lesson to the current situation, this becomes a clarion call for citizen action.

There is an enormous power arising from millions of interconnected people striving together towards a shared vision. We already know, within ourselves, what that vision looks like. In contrast to Trump's intolerance based on a rhetoric of separation, the foundation of a flourishing future is our intrinsic connectedness: within ourselves, with others, and with the natural world.

Pioneers of a flourishing future have already been busily constructing a coherent platform of alternative ideas that can form the framework for a system founded on compassionate values.

We're just entering the abyss, and no-one can predict how bad it's going to get. But as we move together into the darkness, along with our anguish and outrage, let us never lose sight of the light that lurks beyond. There will be casualties from his brutality. Few of us are likely to make it through unscathed. But by recognizing the power of our interconnected action, while keeping our gaze focused on the light beyond the horizon, we may well succeed in ultimately directing this tipping point away from collapse, and towards a society of flourishing, compassion, and justice."

https://patternsofmeaning.com/2016/12/20/towards-the-tipping-point-understanding-trump-in-a-larger-historical-context/

7. RESISTANCE IS FERTILE

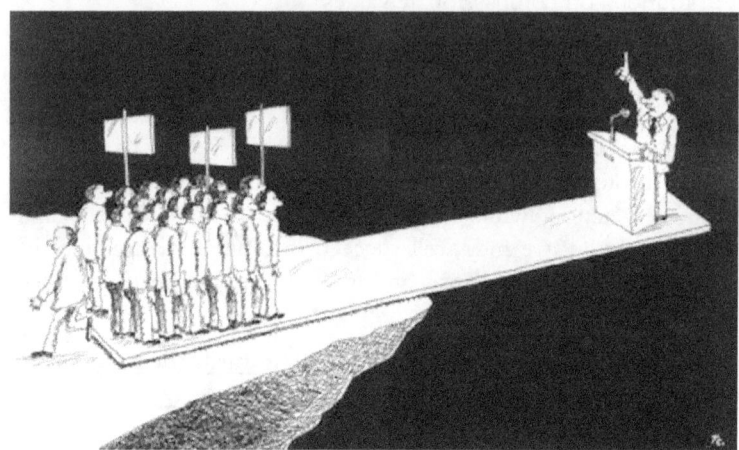

Figure 4: Resistance is fertile

"The system will collapse if we refuse to buy what they are selling – their ideas, their version of history, their wars, their weapons, their notions of inevitability. Remember this: we be many and they be few. They need us more than we need them. Another world is not only possible, she is on her way. On a quiet day, I can hear her breathing."

Arundhati Roy

Detaching from the System

Maddy Harland is the editor of my favourite magazine, *'Permaculture, Practical Solutions Beyond Sustainability'*. She asked a panel of theologists and farmers how they thought we might grow consciousness, because she believes that a growth in consciousness is the mechanism to begin a paradigm shift to a more resilient, regenerative and kinder world.

"To paraphrase the answers: we are living at a time that resembles 1933 in terms of the rise of the Far Right and the brutality of neoliberalism. Corporations without ethics, industrial agriculture, land grabbing, and the disenfranchisement of the peasantry are rife globally. These are powerful forces. It is essential that we, who represent regenerative, healing, sustainable, enlightened, ethical practices, support each other and speak out in the world. We must not be inert. We are called to be radical. We can create change by engaging our heads with our hearts and then acting from that place. It is of great importance to nurture our love and connection with the Earth, to treat it as sacred in our daily practice, and devise ways of sharing insights and practical actions as widely as possible, whether we are a farmer, horticulturalist, Gardner, policymaker, teacher, parent...

Your belief system is your personal choice. I'm not prescribing or projecting anything onto you. What I am suggesting is that irrespective of belief, let's help each other to become the people we want to be. Let's develop our own practices that bring us closer to nature, more capable of listening and reflecting, more supportive of each other, and more able to act with greater wisdom and good effect in the world."

Maddy Harland

Despite what we have been told about 'austerity', there is still enough for everyone. The earth can provide an abundance of food, energy, natural medicine, and building supplies that can easily meet the needs of everyone. If you believe this then it is easy to see how the slogan popularised by Karl Marx might work: '*From each according to her ability, to each according to her needs'*.

Humans are the only beings who have to pay to be on the Earth but in reality the Earth does not charge us money for anything. It is our artificial economic system that creates lack and scarcity in order to run a slave civilization.

"Nature gives us everything for free, nature doesn't charge us any money, all nature asks of us is that we protect it."

Indigenous wisdom.

So we continue to kill ourselves and our world with poison food, toxic water, and polluted air, not to mention depression, anxiety, poverty and a host of other socio-economic issues – all caused or related to the global economic system. Its easy to blame corrupt world leaders, governments, corporations and a host of other problematic sources – but the system continues because we agree to it. We have even started to set up world leaders as pantomime villains like Trump, so we can all point the finger at our own shadow and once again remain ineffective agents of change in ourselves.

Perhaps, our implicit agreement with this system is complacent, but our agreement with it and operation of it perpetuates the crime. Are you part of the problem, or part of the solution? It is not enough to hand over responsibility and to perform the sham of an imaginary democratic event, voting every few years to change just the faces in a pro-economic system killing our world for money.

We are trapped in this system that operates through our conditioned beliefs in separation, competition, scarcity, unworthiness, fear of loss, victimhood and powerlessness, which are all related to our survival. Anyone or anything that activates these survival based beliefs can easily manipulate us – provoking lower vibration beliefs. Activating these causes fear-based reactions that keep us imprisoned in negative thought and action patterns.

For example, if you have a belief that there is not enough to go around, you become competitive to get your piece of the pie. If you did not believe in scarcity or competition, you would not make the same choices in your life or teach your children to make those choices.

In order to keep the system running you must also believe that your survival is solely dependent upon the system, including your right to live in your home, your food, health and general well-being. In order to maintain this negative belief, you must completely forget that the source of all things is infinite and abundant – and it does not cost any money.

Corporations, world leaders and governments are the controllers. They take what is given from nature and they monetize it and monopolise it – so that we look toward them as our false-gods, and we give all our power away. If you look to the controllers for the source of your survival, you allow them to manipulate you. They do this by feeding the negative beliefs of our ego-selves, via means of media, education, propaganda and a host of other artificial sources endemic in all of our social systems.

For example, the mass-media news reinforces separation, competition, scarcity powerlessness and victimhood. Forget about the actual stories and simply notice the beliefs that are being fed – over and over again. In fact, almost everywhere you look you get the same message. A fear-based society is an easy society to control so they must do whatever it takes to keep us asleep by activating our already ingrained disempowering beliefs. These unquestioned stories run very deep.

But if we stop allowing these control stories to be fed to us and choose to release these beliefs the fabric of our reality will change. The thought comes first because our beliefs create our reality. In order to heal our world we must release beliefs that create a negative fear-based reality and claim beliefs that support a reality based on love, kindness and abundance.

So the first point of resistance is psychological. We free ourselves by releasing disempowering beliefs, and embracing beliefs that are aligned with our highest good. Our ability to create a different reality through our beliefs is infinitely more powerful than any artificial power that operates in the world.

Try on a few:

- I am not a victim so I will not give my power and freedom to a government to 'protect me'

- I am worthy so I do not need a social system that asks me to prove my worth. I speak up, stand out, and am true to myself because I do not need to 'fit in' to a society

- I enjoy supporting others in their success because I value co-operation over competition

- I am part of you and you are part of me

- We are part of the world and relinquish our separation

- I relinquish any dependence on a system that keeps me enslaved

The controlling stories and their perpetuators need us to believe that we are powerless, unworthy, needy, potential victims in order to keep us compliant, but every single one of those beliefs is a lie.

"When a well-packaged web of lies has been sold gradually to the masses over generations, the truth will seem utterly proposterous and its speaker a raving lunatic."

Dresden James

It is your responsibility to heal your own piece of the puzzle. *'Think global and act local'* is a great slogan – don't try and take it all on – it will make your shoulders ache! You can start to change our socioeconomic system by healing yourself of false beliefs, such as victimhood, powerless, loss and unworthiness. You heal false beliefs by turning your attention away from them and turning your attention to a higher truth. All healing is a release of false belief. It requires time, intention and commitment, but it has never been so easy to heal or release disempowering beliefs, because now there are so many of us doing it.

When you release the old dysfunctional paradigm and reclaim your worth and your power to consciously create, you naturally make different choices that move toward love and connection, and as a result, reality begins to change in ways that support the thriving of a whole new reality.

'Detaching from the System' with thanks to Nanice Ellis, based on 'Wake Up World'

http://humansarefree.com/2015/02/how-to-release-ego-transform-world.html

All Our Actions Are Political

Every single thing we do has political ramifications. Sorry to get all basic on you, but consider your morning dump. Where does it go? What happens to it? What processes are you supporting when you 'put your shit out into the world?' Does it get flushed away down a pipe to be processed at a plant somewhere? The frothy, chocolate milkshake influent usually gets processed into 99% 'clean' effluent to enter the water cycle again. Whatever you put in your body becomes part of this process. Thousands of pharmaceuticals in use globally have potent effects on wildlife and ecosystems, through water. The effluent from contraceptive pills is sometimes at higher levels than in someone actually taking it, often mutating freshwater fish.

The average person produces 50 litres of excrement and 500 litres of urine every year. Chemicals such as sodium chloride, potassium chloride, citric acid and chlorine dioxide are used in used in the water purification. Huge amounts of water are also used to process the effluent. In the US and 10% of the UK fluoride is also added to drinking water, apparently in a mass-medication to prevent tooth decay (this has never been medically proven), although you may find darker reasons attributed to this. The fluoride sometimes added to municipal water supplies is a toxic byproduct from the fertilizer industry from where it is purchased.

The addition of chlorine to drinking water causes large molecular clusters which don't penetrate deep into the body, leaving people dehydrated and acidified. A morning poop supports all this!

Perhaps you have a septic tank where all your excrement sits and bubbles away until pumping-out time, with the liquid element leaching out into the land. The lorry that pumps it out still takes it to the processing plant. Perhaps you have an electric loo that cooks your turds to a crispy dryness, removing all of the germs. Like processing plants, much of the 'finished product' makes its way back to land as a fertiliser.

Have you ever used a composting toilet? In these, the urine and faeces streams are sometimes separated, the solids going into a bucket that breaks down over a couple of years, mixed with organic material such as wood chippings. The liquids run off into the land or are collected to enhance compost. The finished product is returned to the land, often full of mushrooms, to feed trees (rather than on the vegetable garden). Perhaps you just poop in a hole and cover it up? Then grow a tree?

These poop scenarios are choices and each has a different consequence. One difference between an 'awake' person and one who is still sleeping is about how 'conscious' these choices are. OK you might think it a step too far to say that even taking a shit is a political action, but I don't think it is because I like to think I accept responsibility for my shit.

This is where 'resistance' comes in. A big part of resistance is making conscious choices. That lovely 'tiger loaf' that you enjoy from the supermarket – do you know its made with palm oil? In consuming this you are supporting the destruction of the habitat of Orangutans? Eating those Mexican Tacos or the Cornflakes made from genetically modified corn is supporting Monsanto's attack on life, that weedkiller you use that kills bees, your choice of having a cat that kills the local birds, driving to work, using a patio heater ...need I go on?

Becoming 'awake', becoming conscious of the consequences of our actions is not easy. It means taking responsibility for our own existence rather than giving it to the lecturer, the doctor, the politician, the government or the system. The real revolution is the revolution of values, and in the end it is only a choice between fear and love.

"If we choose to, we can generate collaborative abundance for all. The first step is to pause and ask: What if we choose collaboration and regeneration over exploitation and degeneration? What if we choose to thrive together, rather than compete against?"

Daniel Christian Wahl

Below are actions you might take to help detach yourself from what some people like to call 'The Matrix':

Personal Actions to Detach from the System

- spend time alone in nature

- grow a garden and eat what it produces

- make your own clothes, furniture and art and crafts

- make love and compassion your default position rather than fear

- explore altered states of consciousness and meditation

- exist fully and consciously in the moment whenever you can

- inform yourself about the real actions of government because they do not tell the truth

- question the official narratives at every opportunity

- spoil your vote

- give yourself space to prioritise inner and outer realms equally

- learn to detach from the ego, be honest, cool, kind and compassionate

- minimise your personal carbon count (eg: http://footprint.wwf.org.uk/)

- protest and resist things that you feel unhappy about

- be aware of where you put your hard-earned money / energy

- examine yourself and your actions closely for signs of the wetiko mass virus

- avoid resources that have been imported where possible

- use creativity, skill and work rather than technology and materials

- design and make (above purchase) things for for durability and repairability

- avoid all forms of fossil fuel use

- avoid fast food outlets

- avoid shopping at large, corporately controlled stores

- turn off the channels of mass communication & create your own news stream and entertainment

- divest from money, refuse to earn enough to pay taxes

- limit your use of the money system to cash or debit card, avoid using credit and don't borrow money

- examine your life and consider more co-operative ways of living

- produce food in your house (eg sprouting seeds, nut milk, yoghurt, kefir etc)

- reduce, reuse, recycle, repair and refuse when you can

Interpersonal and Group Actions to Detach

- barter or exchange goods, shop in locally owned stores or start a food co-op with your neighbours

- bring politics into conversation & be open & concerned

- connect with people and develop forms of group expression

- produce real physical products and sell or exchange them locally

- share stuff with some of your neighbours

- help people overcome denial and accept that the world has changed

- disconnect from power structures & hegemonies

- refuse to earn enough money to pay taxes

- make good new stories about people on the earth and tell them to people

- start or join a Local Economic Trading System (LETS)

- join or create a Local Credit Union

Being in the moment

Our government, and increasing ourselves, sometimes seem to exist to just to service the national debt and become full-time bean counters, justifying every action and every moment financially. The curse of 'money consciousness' is that it removes us from existing in the moment. We are either justifying our existence to the 'system' in some way, or planning how to purchase the next object of desire, or just get by. Money clearly puts us in the past or the future, never in the now. This is how consciousness of money destroys our ability to enjoy life.

Life has far more to offer. Joy, fun, transcendence, laughter, love; all the human things that make life worth living exist *in the moment* and we are blessed with hundreds of ways to find that moment. How do you want to spend your precious moments on this Earth?

So put the accounts away for a while, forget about the guilt of your wealth and go out to connect with the Universe, (unless of course 'accounting' is your thing!) Existing in the moment is extremely rewarding and utterly good for you! Here are twelve suggestions from my own personal favourites:

1. **Growing, making, eating food**. From planting the squash seeds, nurturing the little plants, watching them romp across the beds, enjoying the huge yellow flowers and the pleasure they give the bees, staring in rhapsody at the unique fruits they produce to the delight of picking, cooking and eating them, it is an experience without comparison.

Eating food, like sex, is one of the very few activities which employ all of the senses and can be completely transcendent. I'm not saying I had sex with the squashes, but they were damn beautiful. 'Growing your own' puts you in touch with nature and its rhythms and seasons, increasing your awareness and contact with nature and the universe.

2. **Physical work with nature**. I find something as simple as sawing wood, mucking out a stable or digging soil to be an intensely pleasurable experience. It is so 'clean'. You harvest the wood, you get warm. You saw the wood (no chainsaws here), you get warm again. You burn the wood – you get warm again in front of the fire. I have had many moments over the years where, totally absorbed in physical work with nature, lost for a time, transcended, I 'come too' and re-discover myself as an independent entity. Just sheer physical enjoyment of your body, your 'animal' nature, in sport or play or work can tune you into the universe.

3. **Craft activity**. Making things with your hands is also a way to become one with the universe. You can see this in pottery, knitting, watercolour painting and a whole host of art and craftwork where the creator has 'transcended' and become a vessel directly channelling the energies of the universe into the material through their own unique physiology. It is nothing short of fantastic when this happens to you and for a short moment you become 'the one'.

4. **Practising a sense of wonder**. A sky full of stars never fails to move me. Get yourself to a place without light pollution and spend some time enjoying them. The Milky Way unfurled like a huge ribbon across the sky and uncountable pinpricks of twinkling lights glittering above. Excuse me while I wax rhapsodic but if you consciously realise each one of those pinpricks of light is another sun then that pretty

quickly puts things in perspective. You are Nothing. The Universe is Infinite. Simply expand your nothingness into infinity ! There you go !

5. **Enjoying time with children and animals**. Children, dogs, cats and other animals are quite naturally 'in the moment'. Join in with their world and play their games with them. Pretty soon you will discover a universe of fun filled hours covered in mud.

6. **Sports**. Another way to spend fun filled hours covered in mud, many sports can help you to connect with a sense of 'one-ness' through sheer physicality. From one-ness achieved through 'Zen and the Art of Archery' (mastery of craft, skill, sport) to the natural endorphins released through physical exertion. The more you put in, the more you get out – sports can leave you not only feeling (and looking) fit, but give you a deep connection and a feeling of unity.

7. **Dancing**. I used to enjoy 'freelance' dancing but someone turned me on to Salsa a few years ago and I found a suitable class. Discovering this dance led me to book my only ever long-haul flight I have taken to go to Cuba to learn from the natives.

Talk about pure existence in the moment – I love dancing Salsa like nothing else. Maybe Salsa isn't your dance but there are so many different forms of dance there is just bound to be one that suits you.

8. **Making music**. I have got this far writing this list and suddenly feel utterly blessed, because I can play the guitar. How many times has making music helped me transcend the everyday mundanity of 'necessary' existence. Music is a pure form of energy and creating it, even listening to it, can take you into another dimension. Through music you can transcend ordinary reality and become one with a universe of energy. Like dancing, there are many forms of music and many ways to create it. Percussive music, such as drumming can be deeply transformative, to strings to wind… Go on a search to 'find your instrument' and use it as a key to open the universe around you.

Singing, like music, has the power to transform not just yourself but those around you. Those of you lucky enough to have good voices, please sing more often. Those of you who are not so sure maybe sing to yourselves more. Or you could get some help or even adopt an instrument. Humming can be pretty good too. Harmonica anyone ?

9. **Tantra**. When I first discovered Tantra for myself, my friend claimed to be a Tantrika but resolutely refused to tell me what it was about. So I enrolled on a weekend course. It was simply the most amazing experience and completely beyond description. I have been on other courses with other teachers since then. It's not what you think it is. It defies description. Go find out for yourself.

10. **Loving relationships**. Following on from the last, your partner (if you have one to love) is a gateway to the universe. Through union with another it is a short step to union with everything. Religions are very poor at letting you know this.

11. **Mixing with elemental forces**. Filled with awe at the Grand Canyon (earth), amazed at the stars (air / space), lost in the playful flames or relaxed by the rhythm of ocean waves – the elements in their raw state have a profound effect on a being open to their influence. Find raw elemental places in tune with your being and go to them to surrender yourself. Even create a ritual in which you combine the elements, for example building a chimney of rock with a fire in the middle as the tide comes in.

12. **Meditation**. To an extent all of the above are forms of 'dynamic' meditation. Many people practice Yoga, Tai chi, Qigong and other more formal forms of mediation and if this suits you it is a great way to open yourself to other ways of being 'connected'.

The universe is always there, always waiting for us to be in it. The culture in which we exist seems contrived to separate us from being one with the universe. We do have a choice.

Forms of Resistance and Protest

Intellectual self-defense is a useful personal attribute in an Age of Insanity. There are many persuasion techniques to, for example, help someone overcome denial. The dominant narrative has all sorts of entrenched ideology, neatly summarised below by Wendell Berry. The assumptions he lists are the basis of 'wetiko capitalism' and need to be questioned at every turn.

"The Global 'free market' economy is inherently an enemy to the natural world, to human health and freedom, to industrial workers, and to farmers and others in land-use economies; and furthermore, that it is inherently an enemy to good work and good economic practice.

I believe that this perception is correct and that it can be shown to be correct merely by listing the assumptions implicit in the idea that corporations should be free to buy low and sell high in the world at large.

These assumptions, so far as I can make them out, are as follows:

1. That stable and preserving relationships among people, places and things do not matter and are of no worth.

2. That cultures and religions have no legimate practical or economic concerns.

3. That there is no conflict between the 'free market' and political freedom, and no connection between political democracy and economic democracy.

4. That there can be no conflict between economic advantage and economic justice.

5. That there is no conflict between greed and ecological or bodily health

6. That there is no conflict between self interest and public service.

7. That the loss or destruction of the capacity anywhere to produce neccessary goods does not matter and involves no cost.

8. That it is alright for a nation's or a region's subsistence to be foreign based, dependent on long-distance transport, and entirely controlled by corporations.

9. That, therefore, wars over commodities - our recent Gulf War for example - are legimate and permanent economic functions.

10. That this sort of sanctioned violence is justified also by the predominance of centralised systems of production supply, communications and transportation which are extremely vulnerable not only to acts of war between nations, but also to sabotage and terrorism.

11. That it is alright for poor people in poor countries to work for poor wages to produce goods for export to affluent people in rich countries.

12. That there is no danger and no cost in the proliferation of exotic pests, weeds and diseases that accompany international trade and that increase in the volume of trade.

13. That the economy is a machine, of which the people are merely the interchangeable parts. One has no choice but to do the work (if any) that the economy prescribes, and to accept the prescribed wage.

14. That, therefore, vocation is a dead issue. One does not do the work that one chooses to do because one is called to do it by Heaven or by one's natural or God given abilities, but does instead the work that is determined and imposed by the economy. Any work is all right as long as one gets paid for it."

Extracted from Global Problems. Local Solutions, Wendell Berry. Resurgence No. 206

Charlemagne was also known as Charles the Great, and was king of the Franks between 768 and 814, and emperor of the West between 800 and 814. He founded the Holy Roman Empire, strengthened European economic and political life, and promoted the cultural revival known as the Carolingian Renaissance. He proclaimed that *"To have another language is to possess a second soul."*

This is because so many of our understandings are ingrained into our culture at the level of its written and spoken language that they can dictate our thoughts.

Brushing up on discussion techniques is essential if you want to argue the irrational values of corporate consumerism. It may be possible to persuade people into thinking other thoughts and taking other actions. My personal feeling is though, that there is little to be gained from arguing. What we need is a language of the heart.

Identifying some of the false arguments as presented below may help soften a person's entrenched position. I have put some other more complex examples of undefined language uses and how to challenge them into '**Appendix 2, Language Meta Models'** in the back of this book as they may not be everyone's 'cup of tea!'

Ad Hominem: attacking the person's character rather than the argument

Straw Man Fallacy: misrepresenting an argument in order to make it easier to attack

Hasty Generalisation: using small numbers or single examples to represent the all

Begging the Question: Prove a proposition based on a false premise

Post Hoc / False Cause: Claiming that because something happened before it must be the cause

False Dichotemy: Reducing the argument down to two possibilities

Ad Ignorantum: Claiming that because you are ignorant it must be true

Burden of Proof Reversal: Laying the burden of proof onto the one questioning the claim. Also called 'Gish Gallop', a favourite of Trump's

Non Sequiter: Assuming 'this' follows 'that' when there is no logical connection

Bandwagon Fallacy: Just because people think it is so doesn't mean it is true

Because our language is so tied up with the ways we are persuaded to think, it is very important to question these 'linguistic pre-emptions' to get at the truth. There are many ways to counter the imposition of false stories and myths that condition us to behave as slaves. However – meaningful dialectic just isn't what it used to be when people invest their egos in entrenched positions and refute everything that doesn't support their belief systems.

It is very easy to find new stories for yourself when even just growing food, foraging, knitting clothes or making your own stuff have all become acts of resistance to corporate control. I love it that growing my own food and knitting hats is an act of resistance. It makes picking hazelnuts and blackberries so much more exciting!

Art resistance. As someone who took a Degree level course in 'Art and Design in a Social Context' at Dartington College of Arts, this, of course, is one of my favourite forms of resistance. Capturing community expressions through murals has moved on 1000 miles since I went to art college and now there are some brilliant, highly political and subversive artworks around. In truth this subject is a book or two in itself. There are hundreds of public examples, but here's just one from 'Liberate Tate':

"Liberate Tate is an art collective that makes unsanctioned live art in Tate spaces to free Tate from BP. On the 11th March 2016, Tate announced BP sponsorship would end. Today Liberate Tate celebrates this victory for the gallery, the public, artists and the environment and makes the following artists' statement:

"Thank you everyone for coming here today. There will be no speeches. There will be no naming of names. Instead, THIS is our artists' statement.

This is a day many thought would never come. BP sponsorship of Tate is inevitable, they said. BP sponsorship of Tate is vital, they said. Without it, Tate could not function, they said. That's just the way it is, they said. But we changed that. You changed that. We all did this.

We did this with our determination, commitment, stamina, tenacity, audacity, outrage, creativity, artistic craft, deep ecology and soulful collaboration. We did this with approximately 75 litres of molasses, 25 litres of sunflower oil, 20 helium balloons, 15 whispered hours of court transcripts, 1 tonne of arctic ice, 50 tubes of black paint, one 16.5 metre wind turbine blade, 1 portable toilet, 20 black sleeping sacks, 600 sticks of willow charcoal, 60 carefully selected texts, 60 millilitres of black tattooing ink, 600 black latex gloves, and 100 or so black veils – including one at 64 square metres.

We did this together. We did this with Art. We did this as Art.

We stayed true to a collective, collaborative artistic practice to create porous, participatory performances that were genuinely confrontational. We honoured artists like the Guerilla Girls, Hans Haacke and Joseph Beuys in our work, and we referenced activist movements like Climate Camp and Occupy in our activities. We were always inside Tate, talking to staff, working with the support of the PCS Union, bringing our questions from the outside world into the heart of the gallery.

BP continues to attempt to mine the tar sands in Canada. BP continues to face legal challenges from Colombian farmers and Louisiana fisherfolk. BP continues to benefit from its associations with the National Portrait Gallery, the Royal Opera House and the British Museum. Our work is not done.

Yet, Tate is liberated from BP. Tate is liberated.

We end with the words of Doreen Massey, who sadly passed away one week ago today, who supported and inspired our work. She wrote these words when Tate Modern was opened in the year 2000: "Within London, Tate Modern marks a new assertiveness. From the restaurant you can stare the city and St. Paul's more equally in the eye. The challenge is to combine this reborn centrality with a real embeddedness in place – and to preserve within its new-found authority that old ability, on occasions, to cock a snook at the powers that be." By ejecting BP, Tate has indeed cocked a snook at BP, at the fossil fuel industry, at the British establishment and those in the art world that hold back progress.

We look forward to seeing galleries and museums around the world follow this lead in the months and years to come. For a fossil free culture! Free art from oil!"

Go take a look here: http://www.liberatetate.org.uk/

Art and activism does not usually employ 'representational art' but organizes activists and artists through radical and transformative friendships to create works of insurrectionary imagination. It helps to organize social movements to meaningful and effective expression.

You can involve yourself at a collective level in making art, and there are plenty of instructional videos online to help you with this. You can also 'go it alone'. Just recognise your own feelings and let them lead you into expressing them in a local way, in your way, through your art. What actions might you take?

Here are three practical examples of 'art resistance' from my own activity which I have written-up for you. Choose your acts of resistance from your own skill sets and let creative unhappiness guide you. What really makes you mad and what might you do about it as a form of artistic expression?

1. Re-labelling: This product kills bees

With a long, cold winter in the UK this year, on top of a summer last year which was pretty hard on wildlife, bees are having a difficult time and populations are dropping severely. As if the Varroa Mite was not enough on top of this – some pesticides regularly used in the UK contain neonicotinoid, which is also proven to kill bees. Their populations across the UK are getting decimated, yet they are responsible for cross-pollinating at least a third of the plants from which us humans eat the produce. It is estimated, that without bees – human beings would die out within five years or so as there would be no cross pollination of plants.

Added to that, all species on this planet have as much right to exist as we do. It is essential that humans stop destroying other species and cultures through their short sighted greed.

In what can only be described as an utterly cynical marketing campaign, ASDA were selling bee-killing neonicotinoid pest sprays – but promoting their sale by giving away free packets of 'bee friendly' garden plant seeds.

This annoyed me enough to produce some free sticker layouts that you are welcome to download and print onto self-adhesive stickers to 'correct' this disinformative marketing ploy in ASDA and other shops and gardening centres that abandon responsibility to the environment in preference to profit.

Simply stick these stickers onto products in shops that kill bees, in order to inform other customers who might not realize that this is what they are doing by purchasing the product.

Disclaimer: I cannot of course endorse any illegal activity and in itself, providing you with the bullets for an anti-disinformation campaign, in the form of these stickers, is not illegal. However, placing stickers onto products in shops may well lead to your prosecution if you should get caught and I am making it quite clear here that I cannot be held responsible and that the choice of such action is made by you entirely.

Figure 5: Bee sticker book of 90 stickers

Comments:

Roger says: *"What a great idea!!*

These stickers look friendly but at the same time they make people aware of the danger of pesticides. Really: great idea!!! Thanks!"

Erica says: *"I love this. Thank you. I work at a garden center here in the US and should be able to easily covert these stickers on, with my back up verbal education - one gardener at a time."*

Gary says: *"Hi, Great idea indeed, we shared this on our social media channels and our readers thought so as well. We also mentioned this on our recent beekeeping podcast."*

Lorri says: *"Excellent idea, Thank You. I have reposted this to Facebook ."*

Betsy says: *"I blogged about this today and added links back to your article and stickers. Way to go! Love this idea!"*

2. Make a Kayapo Headdress

I am so unhappy at the way that the exigencies of 'economy' continue to treat the indigenous peoples of this planet. The Masai in Africa, a spectacularly beautiful people who are being driven off their ancestral lands to benefit game hunters. The Lakota Indians of North America who are having their sacred heartlands sold off to the highest bidder, most likely for commercial development. But most of all, the Kayapo and other tribes of the Xingu River in the Amazon Basin who are being driven from a sustainable life of freedom, in tune with nature, to one which is a million miles away in terms of anything they might want or desire. A life out of touch with nature.

Again and again, relentlessly, the force of greed, of money, drives civilised, gentle, earth-loving and sustainable societies to destruction. Aborigines to alcoholics, smallpox infested blankets for the 'redskins', even some of the 'Cornish', where I live in Cornwall talk about 1000 years of English genocide. I hate this about our supposed 'civilisation', that it still so clearly destroys innocence and beauty and 'other ways' of living on this earth, so often without even noticing them. It makes me ashamed to be part of the system that espouses this.

I am not alone here and the case of the Amazon Xingu tribes is what inspired James Cameron to create the most brilliant environmental film ever; Avatar. Years ago in 1989, I bought a book called '*Jungle Stories: The Fight for the Amazon*', written by Sting and Jean-Pierre Dutilleux about their visit to the Kayapo tribe where they stayed with Chief Raoni. I still have it and in the intervening 30 years or so years since describing the problems so clearly, the situation of the indigenous tribes has got far worse, with clear mass-murder, poisoning, environmental destruction, illegal mining and logging and land clearance for livestock and dam building now being commonplace.

It makes me mad. I mean really angry and twisted inside and I think this is because I feel so powerless to do anything to help them beyond the life choices I already make. With Jair Bolsonaro as the president of Brazil the situation for the indigenous people's of the rainforest gets even more desperate.

So it came to me that I should make a Kayapo head dress and wear it to show my sympathy with these tribes, and to, in some small way, promote more awareness of what seems to be a virtual news embargo on the genocide being caused by the economic interests of consumerism and its greed for exploiting other people's land for materials and energy. I can hear the accusations of 'cultural misappropriation' already, but it is just, not.

It is very easy to make one of these head-dresses, all you need are some good size feathers of whatever type takes your fancy. In this example I have used dyed goose feathers. For the headband I used an old leather belt that I cut, along the belt, into strips. I made holes most of the way along about three quarters of the way up, with an auger, and pushed feathers through the holes from the 'outside' to the 'inside', which gives them an outward pointing 'crown' effect. On the inside I had previously put some heavy-duty, double-sided sticky tape. Once all the feathers were through I stripped of the top layer of the tape and bedded the feathers onto it, making sure that they were all front-faced, which gives a nice convex curve to the crown of feathers.

Above the holes where the feathers stick through, the belt bends inwards, helping thrust the feathers slightly outwards rather than straight up. I stuck the other bit of belt on top of the feather stems on the inside of the hat and sealed the bottom join with red insulation tape to match colours.

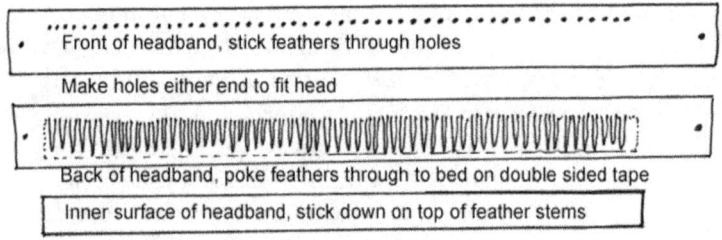

Figure 6: Diagram for headdress assembly

So some purchased goose feathers and old leather belt with carpet tape might not be very indigenous but this achieved something that looks pretty much like a Kayapo head dress to me. A bit of make up and I feel somewhere between a person sympathising with the Kayapo and a member of the Village People. I know some people will want to say 'This is just cultural appropriation', but I believe not. This is coming from a genuine place.

Figure 7: Kayapo style head dress made with goose feathers

Comments:

Jothee says: *"Hi, this is a powerful piece on the people of the world holding on to a way of living only the affluent and super rich can have, whereas the common man of any of the continents is struggling to find bread. I have met a few maasais as I come from Kenya who are in Europe and the Americas working and living under cruel conditions working menial jobs just so that they can send something back to their homes for those they left behind after they were forcefully removed from their heritage land.*

Concerning the head-dress — WEAR IT every eye brow raised will lead to another. Is also possible to republish this article on my blog the website above. Keep on spreading in love and debate!!"

June says: *"I have goose feathers… gonna dye them. thanks for this… a family reunion is coming up. I spent 4 months in Brazil spent one week with a Xanvante tribesman. Love the people. Currently reading Martin Prechtel's Stealing Beneficios Roses. Also read Secrets of the Talking Jaguar and Long Life, Honey in the Heart. Martin writes so very eloquently about the indigenous. Thanks for your input."*

Stephenie writes: *"I am so happy to see this. I am sure my students will be interested in this and I can connect their learning about indigenous people, in Hawaii, our home, and worldwide, to the reading, math and writing standards we are using. Mahalo!"*

Eva says: *"I will join you by making a Kayapo headdress and I will wear it. And I will teach others to do the same."*

Kirsteen says: *"Wear it, yes indeed. k x x"*

Nova says: *"I happened across your article while looking for pictures or kayapo headdress styles. I am Taino from Boriken, we also wear kayapo style headdresses, small crowns like yours and really long ones consisting of hundreds of feathers.*

I like that you made yours the way you did. I did something similar with macaw feathers, leather and glue, when first rediscovering my tribes headdresses many years ago. Eventually I learned to make them traditionally using only feathers and string, and have been making them since. Very cool story, thanks for sharing."

3. Guerilla gardening: Seedbomb Christmas

From 'The Anarchists Garden'. When it came to making Christmas presents this year with the resources I had on hand – I found I had the stuff to make and package some rather nice Seed Bombs.

I had some old Raku clay which had been sitting around in a bucket, and mixed it half and half with some compost, liberated from the tomato plants that had ended. I also added some wood ash from the woodburner and some sawdust to bulk it up a bit, and also to help the bombs break down once they got wet in the spring.

Once I was happy with the consistency I divided the pile of mix into four. To each quarter of the mix I added a generous portion of single seed from the garden and just enough water (with food colourant for ID) to make it maleable. Then I set about mashing the mix up to make the clay element 'plastique' enough to hand roll the balls. I set them by the fire in the evening and re-rolled each one to make them smoother, marking each ball according to its contents.

It is important to dry the balls quickly without overheating, so as not to roast the seed or leave it damp for so long it germinates. After four evenings by the fire I thought that these seedbombs were dry enough to package for Christmas presents. I had a load of old postage tubes left over from an earlier project and cut these in half to take eight bombs in each, two of each seed variety, then dreamed up a nice bit of labelling for the tubes, each of which said:

"Best thrown in late spring, onto open soil if possible. Invented by the father of the 'One Straw Revolution', Masanobu Fukuoka for getting seed into inaccessible places. These clay and compost seed-bombs protect the seeds until they are warm and wet enough to grow, then feed them when they start life. Bring nature back to derelict land and oppose the dull monoculture of land exploitation. Four types of seed bombs in each packet."

Since making these seedbombs I have discovered a better mix for them using ground charcoal, seed compost and cornflour. I have also produced hempbombs and am trying to persuade others to do this in order to re-naturalise hemp into what remains of the British countryside.

Figure 8: A cardboard tube of seedbombs

Protesting is a well-established form of resistance and the advent of social media has helped to make protests more effective and easier to organise. Unfortunately the police have developed new, and dangerous practices to limit their effectiveness, such as 'kettling'– cramming protesters into a small area. At the 'Water Protectors' camp in Dakota, protestors have had to endure not only freezing winter temperatures but also rubber bullets, tear gas, water cannons and actions to cut off their food, information and other supplies.

Protest can also take the form of contacting people, businesses, government departments, the ombudsman, supermarket chains and so on to try and change their attitude or practice. It is often surprising how cooperative they can be.

Direct Action and Civil Disobedience are a step on from protesting. In a recent landmark court case in the US, "*The jury recognized the integrity, honor, and patriotism of Ken Ward, and recognized that what he did was done for all of us*," said fellow valve-turner Leonard Higgins.

Offering some hope that 'reality' will prevail in a political climate seemingly bent on climate destruction, a Washington state jury on Wednesday failed to convict activist Ken Ward on two felony counts stemming from an act of civil disobedience against the fossil fuel industry.

The Climate Disobedience Center, which Ward co-founded, declared the mistrial '*a resounding recognition of the threat of climate change,*' noting that one or more jurors refused to convict Ward on charges of sabotage and burglary for breaking into and shutting down a Kinder Morgan pipeline near Anacortes, Washington last year. Alternately, they were persuaded by his argument that he had acted out of necessity, in defense of the planet.

According to the centre, Ward's defense consisted exclusively of his motivation to confront the threat of climate change, and the defense did not contest a single piece of evidence brought by the prosecution. Several exhibits demonstrating climate science and impacts and the role of civil disobedience in societal change were permitted as evidence. Ward himself was the only witness called by the defense. The jury deliberated while looking at charts demonstrating the dramatic increase of greenhouse gasses in the atmosphere and the impacts of sea-level rise to Skagit County.

"*This trial was about climate change*," said Emily Johnston, who also took part in the October 2016 coordinated action that shut down tar sands pipelines along the U.S.-Canada border.

"*The prosecution presented only information about what Ken did on October 11, and Ken and the defense presented only information about climate change, so the only decision that the jury was making was which story mattered more. And the story of the climate crisis won.*"

...Ward was the first of the 'valve turners' to appear in court and the trial was said to have *"far-reaching implications for the widening pipeline protest movement and the intensifying crackdown against it,"* particularly in light of the fierce mobilizations of U.S. President Donald Trump's recent executive orders advancing the controversial Keystone XL (KXL) and Dakota Access (DAPL) pipelines.

As Ward himself explained after the decision,

"In five hours, the jury was unable to decide that with all of the evidence against me, including the video of me closing the valve, that this was a crime. I didn't contest a single piece of the evidence, only presented my story and evidence of catastrophic climate change. This is a tremendous outcome."

As it stands, there will be a conference next week to determine if a new trial will be scheduled. But as Steve Kent with the Climate Disobedience Center explained to Common Dreams, the fact of the mistrial gives

"an indication that one or more jurors accepted the argument that the actions were taken to prevent climate harm, and so weren't culpable. That's important legally and will have ramifications."

Not only does this ruling bode well for the future 'valve turner' trials, but it also could impact other activists who plan to confront the Trump administration with increasingly direct civil disobedience.

"The failure of the prosecution's case shows that public opinion is shifting about the need for direct action to solve the climate crisis," said Kelsey Skaggs, an attorney with the Climate Defense Project, which provided legal support to Ward alongside the Civil Liberties Defense Center. *"With our political leadership failing us, we need more courageous activists like Ken to stand up to the fossil fuel industry and set an example of how normal people can effect change."*

http://www.commondreams.org/news/2017/02/02/just-time-trump-jury-says-defense-planet-no-crime

In the UK, direct actions about fracking have also led to arrests, including that of M.P. Caroline Lucas. Mostly they are thrown out of court by magistrates who think that the police and private security firms have overstepped legal boundaries.

Direct action works quite often as it can focus the 'new' media spotlight on things the 'controllers' don't want you to see, for example the DAPL protest in Dakota USA. The Dakota Access Pipeline is a 1,172-mile-long (1,886 km) underground oil pipeline project in the United States. The route begins in the Bakken shale oil fields in northwest North Dakota and travels in a more or less straight line south-east, through South Dakota and Iowa, terminating at the oil tank farm near Patoka, Illinois.

The pipeline has been controversial regarding its necessity, and potential impact on the environment, especially considering the amount of pipeline spills that occur already. A number of Native Americans in Iowa and the Dakotas have opposed the pipeline, including the Meskwaki and several Sioux tribal nations.

In August 2016, 'ReZpect Our Water', a group organized on the Standing Rock Indian Reservation, brought a petition to the U.S. Army Corps of Engineers in Washington, D.C. and the tribe sued for an injunction. A protest at the pipeline site in North Dakota near the Standing Rock Indian Reservation has drawn international attention. Thousands of people have been protesting the pipeline construction, with confrontations between some groups of protesters and law enforcement, along with disputes over the facts.

Again, multiple arrests and raids by government-employed private security firms are operating in the interests of big business at the taxpayers expense. Although this longstanding protest is infrequently seen on mainstream news, interested Facebook members and other groups have access to reports on what is happening from the source, and even the live stream for these often 'cut' using modern army technologies.

This wasn't just a battle between protestors and corporate power, but one in which the main sources of our news providers collude with government and corporate power in a process of disinformation and misinformation. As in many wars, truth is the first victim.

Extinction Rebellion. Extinction Rebellion is a campaign by the RisingUp network. It aims to promote a fundamental change of our political and economic system to one which maximises well-being and minimises harm. It is a massive, counter cultural, global movement whose time has come. Extinction Rebellion demands:

1. That the Government must tell the truth about how deadly our situation is, it must reverse all policies not in alignment with that position and must work alongside the media to communicate the urgency for change including what individuals, communities and businesses need to do.

2. Good intentions and guidelines won't save the ice caps. The Government must enact legally-binding policies to reduce carbon emissions in the UK to net zero by 2025 and take further action to remove the excess of atmospheric greenhouse gases. It must cooperate internationally so that the global economy runs on no more than half a planet's worth of resources per year.

3. By necessity these demands require initiatives and mobilisation of similar size and scope to those enacted in times of war. We do not however, trust our Government to make the bold, swift and long-term changes necessary to achieve this and we do not intend to hand further power to our politicians. Instead we demand a Citizens' Assembly to oversee the changes, as we rise from the wreckage, creating a democracy fit for purpose.

A commentary from Dr. Claire Wordley: "If that is what we are facing, why are we all carrying on as normal? Well, some people aren't. Extinction Rebellion is a UK-born group committing civil disobedience to protest catastrophic climate breakdown and species extinctions. Springing apparently from nowhere, in November 2018 the group mobilized thousands of people to block bridges, roads, and government departments in London — trying to cause enough disruption to make the British government act on climate. Extinction Rebellion demands that the UK government declare a climate emergency, that the UK go carbon neutral by 2025, and that the decisions on how to go carbon neutral are taken by a citizen's assembly.

With their use of stark hourglass and human skull imagery, their emotive wording, strong demands, and tactics of civil disobedience, Extinction Rebellion activists have raised hackles in many quarters."

https://news.mongabay.com/2018/12/climates-last-stand-why-extinction-rebellion-protesters-are-breaking-the-law-commentary/

Which means Extinction Rebellion is about: Preparing for national non-violent direct actions and civil disobedience to peacefully force the government to take climate change seriously:

- The government to tell the truth and act as if the truth was real

- Climate mobilisation, as if in war

- Aiming for Zero Carbon Britain by 2025

- Demand reduction

- Ecosystem restoration, regenerative agriculture

- Rebuild transport, energy, production infrastructure as carbon neutral

- Citizen Assemblies to plan the transition to a survivable future

At time of writing many groups are setting-up, planning and undertaking actions of civil disobedience to promote the above aims. See https://rebellion.earth/

Lobbying government online is now an established practice, although one wonders quite how effective it is when there are so many vested interests in play and such a lack of honesty. There are now many online setups to request that a topic is 'debated in Parliament' once it reaches 100,000 votes (for all the good that seems to do!)

Recently a vote to 'Prevent Donald Trump from making a state visit to the United Kingdom' went viral and very quickly gained nearly two million votes for a scheduled discussion in Parliament. According to one online article I read, the thought of the Queen having to meet Donald Trump is enough to make her consider abdication, leaving the throne empty for his visit. Sometimes fake news is amusing.

The pressures seem to have delayed his visit to the UK at least. Pictures taken of Theresa May holding hands with Trump very early in his Presidency leave little to the imagination with regards to her intended direction after the red herring of Brexit distracting people from climate emergency for ages. The process of online lobbying however, seems to have little effect on government policy. Big business lobbying government with bags of money seems to have the edge on this one.

Non-compliance. I wrote earlier *'when laws are made to be unjust, civil disobedience is not only justified, it is necessary'*. I am someone who has walked out of a successful lecturing career over a disagreement of new conditions imposed by government legislation. This non-compliance wasn't easy but was the only option I had to avoid literal wage slavery. The legislation they imposed left me with £11 a week to cover £25 a week travel expenses to get to work – with nothing left over for even food!

There are many forms of non-compliance bound up within the idea of the 'straw man identity' – worthy of research at: http://www.yourstrawman.com/

Also very interesting in terms of non-compliance with banks and debt collection agencies: https://www.getoutofdebtfree.org/

Stand upright, make eye contact and say "I do not comply." It feels powerful doesn't it?

Healing Wetiko

Eckart Tolle believes:

"The pollution of the planet is only an outward reflection of an inner psychic pollution; millions of unconscious individuals not taking responsibility for their inner space."

Many of us know that wordly ambition, material aspiration and perpetual growth are a formula for environmental ruin and mass unhappiness, yet our society is led by people who pursue these goals. *"The consuming of another's life* [including the planet's], *for ones own private purpose or profit"* [Jack D Forbes] is something the Cree Indians call 'Wetiko'.

The greed that drives these planet wreckers comes from a deep insecurity. Its like *'there isn't enough to go round so I must take as much as possible – way more than I need in order to feel safe'.* So this desire to possess and own comes from a deep, personal crisis. Through 'status' and the ownership that drives this, it becomes self perpetuating – *'so-and-so has three Rolex watches and I only have two'.*..

The personal meaninglessness of their existence can only be filled by consuming and owning and winning. Once this awful virus/addiction takes over, the hungry ghost will risk decency, integrity, fairness, compassion and humanity in pursuit of their goals. Anneke Lucas, who was a sex slave to Europe's elite at age 6 wrote the following:

"Power addicts, world leaders and corrupt politicians who abuse children are themselves like children who never grew up, driven to power to avoid ever feeling the humiliation of child abuse again, unconsciously seeking revenge from a place of hurt by recycling the abuse. They lack the courage to heal. I believe that the world is more than ever ready to confront its darkness. We have to if we are to survive as a species."

Bit by bit the insecure have taken over running our systems and investing the world with their insecurities, greed and fears. Far from protecting and keeping their citizens safe, the governments of the UK and US are acting on behalf of a collective of sociopathic, even psychopathic industrialists who want to own everything. They act in the interests of economics, which has the opposite effect of creating the optimum conditions for healthy and happy life on earth. The system they promote wants you sick and unhappy. In order to best serve money, the world needs to be a gigantic marketplace in which we are all isolated individuals competing against each other. Fear and hate drives this isolation and undermines our ability to cooperate.

Many people consider humans as a sort of virus or cancer spreading across the face of the planet, consuming and destroying everything in their path. But this is really another form of denial based on low self-esteem. We are not a virus. We are not a cancer. At their best, human beings are utterly fantastic beings of wonder! Our potential as beings is infinite.

So it is fairer to say that there are a large number of people with a kind of psychic virus, a possession by the demons of wetiko, that lets them believe that earth-rape for personal benefit is perfectly acceptable. Perhaps if there were enough of us we could change the status associated with owning wealth to something new – a kind of realisation of sickness like a psychological virus that Paul Levy identifies as 'malignant egophrenia' in his book '*Dispelling Wetiko, Breaking the Curse of Evil.*' But this story, the 'Wetiko Virus' is written into all of our control systems. One big question I have is 'can these people be healed and if so, how?'

"We have to have hope...and we believe in Spirit. That's the only way we can create miracles."

Chief Arvol Looking Horse at DAPL Oceti Sakowin camp.

"No matter what they ever do to us, we must always act for the love of our people and the Earth. We must not react out of hatred against those who have no sense."

John Trudell

There are still many cultures that live within limits on planet earth, sharing and valuing their resources without wasting or exploiting. There are also increasing numbers of people waking up and refusing plunder the planet by using oil products, driving petrol or diesel driven cars, refusing to engage fully with the money system, becoming vegan and so on. There are hundreds of thousands of people who, like you, are looking for ways to live a wholesome life on this earth.

"The ability to recognise oneself in the other and the other in oneself is a deeply democratising experience. Empathy is the soul of democracy...the more empathic the culture, the more democratic its values and governing institutions."

Jeremy Rifkin

The Dalai Lama was once asked if he could summarise his philosophy in five words. Allegedly, he said "I can say it in two words, just 'Be Kind.'" It is certain to me that compassion has a lot to play in the coming changes and that this is perhaps, the hardest route to take.

To summarise the situation. We have hundreds of thousands, if not millions of people who, with their basic needs fulfilled are waking up to the realisation of the infinite potential of human beings in a universe made of energy.

But they are ruled by a governing system without soul, without heart, run by sociopaths interested in gaining control over money at the expense of life itself, destroying the ability for humans to evolve further. Added to this billions of people on earth are still in poverty or live hand-to-mouth.

How do we change this system into one that is fair for all and still allows humans to reach their potential?

"Our deepest fear is not that we are inadequate. Our deepest fear is that we are powerful beyond measure. It is our light, not our darkness that most frightens us. We ask ourselves, Who am I to be brilliant, gorgeous, talented, fabulous? Actually, who are you not to be? You are a child of the Universe.

Your playing small does not serve the world. There is nothing enlightened about shrinking so that other people won't feel insecure around you. We are all meant to shine, as children do. We were born to make manifest the glory that is within us. It is not just in some of us; it is in everyone. And, as we let our own light shine, we unconsciously give other people permission to do the same. As we are liberated from our own fear, our presence automatically liberates others."

Marianne Williamson, A Return To Love: Reflections on the Principles of A Course in Miracles.

8. MAKING THE NEW

"When asked if I am pessimistic or optimistic about the future, my answer is always the same: If you look at the science about what is happening on Earth and aren't pessimistic, you don't understand data. But if you meet the people who are working to restore this earth and the lives of the poor, and you aren't optimistic, you haven't got a pulse. What I see everywhere in the world are ordinary people willing to confront despair, power, and incalculable odds in order to restore some semblance of grace, justice, and beauty to this world."

Paul Hawken

Permaculture

"The greatest change we need to make is from consumption to production, even if it is on a small scale, in our own gardens. If only 10% of us do this, there is enough for everyone".

Bill Mollison – the Father of Permaculture

Permaculture is one of the most transformative influences in the world today. From 'greening the desert' to providing a home-based food system, permaculture design practice gives us a dance with nature in which we let nature lead. Maddy Harland, Editor of Permaculture Magazine defines it as:

"Permaculture is...an innovative framework for creating sustainable ways of living; a practical method for deveoping ecologically harmonius, efficient and productive systems that can be used by anyone, anywhere."

Permaculture Design Courses (PDC's) are springing up in every country, giving people a new way to relate to the planet they live on. The ideas can be applied to all sorts of systems design, including government. The principles are remarkably simple and clean.

Central to permaculture are the three ethics:

- care for the earth

- care for people

- fair share / future care

They form the foundation for permaculture design and are also found in most traditional societies. Here are the 12 principles of permaculture as described by David Holmgren.

1. **Observe and Interact** – *"Beauty is in the mind of the beholder."* By taking the time to engage with nature we can design solutions that suit our particular situation.

2. **Catch and Store Energy** – *"Make hay while the sun shines."* By developing systems that collect resources when they are abundant, we can use them in times of need.

3. **Obtain a Yield** – *"You can't work on an empty stomach."* Ensure that you are getting truly useful rewards as part of the working you are doing.

4. **Apply Self Regulation and Accept Feedback** – *"The sins of the fathers are visited on the children of the seventh generation."* We need to discourage inappropriate activity to ensure that systems can continue to function well. Negative feedback is often slow to emerge.

5. **Use and Value Renewable Resources and Services** – *"Let nature take its course."* Make the best use of nature's abundance to reduce our consumptive behavior and dependence on non-renewable resources.

6. **Produce No Waste** – *"Waste not, want not"* or *"A stitch in time saves nine."* By valuing and making use of all the resources that are available to us, nothing goes to waste.

7. **Design From Patterns to Details** – *"Can't see the forest for the trees."* By stepping back, we can observe patterns in nature and society. These can form the backbone of our designs, with the details filled in as we go.

8. **Integrate Rather Than Segregate** – *"Many hands make light work."* By putting the right things in the right place, relationships develop between those things and they work together to support each other.

9. **Use Small and Slow Solutions** – *"Slow and steady wins the race"* or *"The bigger they are, the harder they fall."* Small and slow systems are easier

to maintain than big ones, making better use of local resources and produce more sustainable outcomes.

10. **Use and Value Diversity** – *"Don't put all your eggs in one basket."* Diversity reduces vulnerability to a variety of threats and takes advantage of the unique nature of the environment in which it resides.

11. **Use Edges and Value the Marginal** – *"Don't think you are on the right track just because it's a well-beaten path."* The interface between things is where the most interesting events take place. These are often the most valuable, diverse and productive elements in the system.

12. **Creatively Use and Respond to Change** – *"Vision is not seeing things as they are but as they will be."* We can have a positive impact on inevitable change by carefully observing and then intervening at the right time.

David Holmgren is best known as the co-originator of the permaculture concept with Bill Mollison, following the publication of Permaculture One in 1978. His passion about the philosophical and conceptual foundations for sustainability which are highlighted in his book, *'Permaculture: Principles and Pathways Beyond Sustainability'* inspired the 'permacultureprinciples.com' website where you can learn more about permaculture and sustainable living.

Permaculture is principally about managing, working with nature and sharing a yield with her. Cultures such as the Amazon Indians do this already. Much of the Amazon is not just forest, but a huge, tended forest garden that the indigenous share with nature. Permaculture offers us a way to save humanity from its own stupidity, but not save our 'civilisation' – which is the cultural expression of that stupidity.

Albert Einstein supposedly said:

"If I had an hour to solve a problem and my life depended on the solution, I would spend the first 55 minutes determining the proper question to ask. For once I know the proper question, I could solve the problem in less than five minutes."

We often seem to be too busy looking for the answers to clearly define the questions. One of the key slogans of permaculture is *'the problem is the solution'*. Everything that you need to know in order solve a problem is there, waiting in a good definition of the problem.

Before I get lost in enthusing about permaculture I will just ask you to go and look at this set of ideas which can transform everything from how you think about where you live to the management of national and global resources. It is happening now!

"A person of courage today is a person of peace. The courage we need is to refuse authority and to accept only personally responsible decisions. Like war, growth at any cost is an outmoded and discredited concept. It is our lives which are being laid to waste. What is worse, it is our children's world which is being destroyed. It is therefore our only possible decision to withhold all support for destructive systems, and to cease to invest our lives in our own annihilation."

Bill Mollison

"Our conscious evolution is an invitation to ourselves, to open to that positive future, to see ourselves as one planet, and to learn to use our powers wisely and ethically for the enhancement of all life on Earth."

Barbara Max Paul Hubbard

New Currencies

"You never change things by fighting the existing reality. To change something, build a new model that makes the existing model obsolete."

Buckminster Fuller

"Problems cannot be solved with the same mind set that created them."

Einstein

Wild economics is where the growing movement to localise our lives materially meets with the emerging desire of people across the world to relate to each other in a much more inspiring and uplifting way. In contrast to monetary economics it is a form of economy that replicates and draws its inspiration from nature, where people can share their gifts with each other in a way that adds fertility to the earth and their local communities. It is devoid of the notions of debt and credit which riddle modern human culture and which are entirely absent from the wilderness. Wild economics is the convergence of permaculture principles with the evolving realm of gift economics and the realignment of the spiritual with the physical. In wild economics there are many currencies. Ethan C Roland asked the questions:

"What would it look like if we redesigned the global financial system using permaculture principles?" and *"What if our financial system looked more like an ecosystem?"* He came up with eight forms of capital. The Oxford American Dictionary states that capital is, 'wealth in the form of money or other assets' and a 'valuable resource of a particular kind.' What forms might these other assets or valuable resources take?

"Social Capital

Influence and connections are social capital. A person or entity who has 'good social capital' can ask favors, influence decisions and communicate efficiently. Social capital is of primary importance in politics, business and community organizing. Capital can be in the form of equity or debt. In social capital, a person can 'owe' favours or decision-making influence to another person or entity.

Material Capital

Non-living physical objects form material capital. Raw and processed resources like stone, metal, timber, and fossil fuels are 'complexed' with each other to create more sophisticated materials or structures. Modern buildings, bridges, and other pieces of infrastructure along with tools, computers and other technologies are complexed forms of material capital.

Financial Capital

We are most familiar with financial capital: money, currencies, securities and other instruments of the global financial system. The current global society focuses enormous amounts of attention on financial capital. It is our primary tool for exchanging goods and services with other humans. It can be a powerful tool for oppression, or (potentially) liberation.

Living Capital

A precious metal dealer who attended both Financial Permaculture courses advises, "Rather than US dollars, measure your wealth in ounces [of gold and silver]!" Recognizing that 'precious' metals are just another form of financial capital, Catherine Austin Fitts recommends that we diversify and 'Measure our wealth in ounces, acres, and hooves.'

Living capital is made up of the animals, plants, water and soil of our land – the true basis for life on our planet. Permaculture design teaches us the principles and practices for the rapid creation of living capital. Permaculture encourages us to share the abundance of living capital rather than the intangible 'wealth' of financial capital.

(Note: 'Natural Capital' could be a synonym for living capital, but the 1999 book, Natural Capitalism, by Hawken et al. focuses more on a slightly updated system of capitalism than on the true wealth of living systems. The current Slow Money movement is also making strides in a similar direction, seeking to transfer financial capital into the living forms of soil, animals, and agriculture).

Intellectual Capital

Intellectual capital is best described as a 'knowledge' asset. The majority of the current global education system is focused on imparting intellectual capital – whether or not it is the most useful form of capital for creating resilient and thriving communities. Having intellectual capital is touted as the surest way to 'be successful'. Science and research can focus on obtaining intellectual capital or 'truth', though it is often motivated by the desire for financial or social capital. For example, 'going to university' is primarily an exchange of financial capital for intellectual capital. It is supposed to prepare people for the rest of their lives in the world.

Cultural Capital

All the other forms of capital may be held and owed by individuals, but cultural capital can only be gathered by a community of people. Cultural capital describes the shared internal and external processes of a community – the works of art and theater, the songs that every child learns, the ability to come together in celebration of the harvest or for a religious holiday. Cultural capital cannot be gathered by individuals alone. It could be viewed as an emergent property of the complex system of inter-capital exchanges that takes place in a village, a city, a bioregion, or nation.

Experiential (or Human) Capital

We accumulate experiential capital through actually organizing a project in our community, or building a strawbale house, or completing a permaculture design. The most effective way to learn anything comes through a blended gathering of intellectual and experiential capital. My personal experience getting a Master's degree at Gaia University showed me that experiential learning is essential for my effective functioning in the world: I was able to do projects instead of take classes, and I'm now collaboratively organizing the local permaculture guild and co-running a successful permaculture design firm.

I can see that human capital is a combination of social, intellectual and experiential capital – all facets of a person that can be gathered and carried in essentially limitless amounts. But there's one more form of capital that a person can gather and carry inside themselves…

Spiritual Capital

Spiritual capital contains aspects of intellectual and experiential capital, but is deeper, more personal and less quantifiable. Most of the world's religions include a concept of 'the great chain of being', a holarchic understanding of existence where spiritual attainment (in this context, the accumulation of spiritual capital) leads to different levels of being.

In spiritual capital, there again enters the concept that capital can be in the form of equity (gathering positive spiritual experience /understanding /attainment) OR in the form of debt.

In some Mayan cultures (like the Tzutujil of Lago Atitlan), a basic understanding of existence is that humans owe a 'spiritual debt' to the magnificent beauty and complexity of existence. According to this worldview, the goal of one's life in the world is to create works of unspeakable beauty and gratitude, thereby repaying the spiritual debt to existence. The Tzutujil also recognize that single human beings can never really be effective at gathering and flowing capital if they are separated from their community."

From Permaculture Magazine No. 68: Ethan C Roland. 'Eight Forms of Capital'.

Gift Economies

Gift economies confirm the addage *'from each according to his ability, to each according to his needs'* in action. As a self-confessed idealist I was quite happy to start giving things to my neighbours – all you need to do apparently to start the revolution.

Unfortunately my neighbours are of the 'wetiko mind' and caused me to feel like they were the ones doing me a favour just by taking them! Gifts of courgettes, jam, mackerel and the like never came back, nothing but the buzzing drone of their lawnmower mowing a tiny lawn for six hours on every sunny Sunday of the summer. Having got that off my chest, I do believe that one way to 'live rich' is by exchanging stuff you have too much of, but only with those of a like mind.

I am a fan of Mark Boyle and his social experiments and books about living. One of his books is '*The Moneyless Manifesto, Live Well, Live Rich, Live Free*', from the blurb: "That we need money to live – like it or not – is a self-evident truism. Right? Not anymore. Drawing on almost three years of experience as '*The Moneyless Man*', Mark Boyle not only demystifies money and the system that binds us to it, he also explains how liberating, easy and enjoyable it is to live with less of it.

In this book, Mark takes us on an exploration that goes deeper into the thinking that pushed him to make the decision to go moneyless, and the philosophy he developed along the way. Bursting with radical new perspectives on some of the vital, yet often unquestioned, pillars of economic theory and what it really means to be 'sustainable' – as well as creative and practical solutions for how we can live more with less – Boyle offers us one of the world's most thought-provoking voices on economic and ecological ideas.

The Moneyless Manifesto explores why making the transition beyond monetary economics is becoming the zeitgeist of the Occupy generation, and how you can participate in the world's only booming economy – the gift economy."

Mark followed this book up with '*Drinking Molotov Cocktails with Ghandi*'and again from the blurb:

"More than ever, people are longing for deep and meaningful change. Another world is not only possible; it is essential. Yet despite our creative and determined efforts to attain social justice and ecological sustainability, our global crises continue to deepen.

In Drinking Molotov Cocktails with Gandhi, bestselling author Mark Boyle argues that our political and economic system has brought us to the brink of climate catastrophe, ransacking ecosystems and unravelling communities for the benefit of the few at the expense of the many. He makes a compelling case that we must 'rewild' the political landscape, as history teaches us that positive social change has always been wrought by movements prepared to use any means available. The time has come for pacifists, revolutionaries, and freedom fighters to work together for the creation of a world worth sustaining. Eloquent, visionary and beautifully written, this incendiary manifesto strikes at the heart of the world's crises and reframes our understanding of how to solve them, signaling a turning point in our journey towards an ecologically just society.

The three R's of the climate change generation — reduce, reuse, and recycle — are long overdue for an upgrade. Welcome to resist, revolt, rewild."

I'm not going to attempt to boil down what Mark says in these books to some kind of flavourless sauce, enough to say – many of the answers we need, and the questions we should be asking, are in there already. Please read them.

Mark had the good sense to build a 'gift economy centre' with a moneyless pub before setting off into his latest adventure, two years without technology, and is at time of writing, accepting messages by letter only.

Real Education

As I wrote earlier, many of our educational institutions have become control devices to instill economic objectives into people. They have lost contact with the whole point of education – to draw out and extend the abilities of the individual in question. Real education starts with you, the individual and your thoughts, values, dreams, ideas and needs. Anything that doesn't is a form of indoctrination.

I had attended a conference on the role of learning for adults and later emailed a senior member of the government body in charge at the time to enquire whether he thought *'the development of human potential'* was part of their educational remit. I was directed to the 'key tasks' which were all related to numbers of people achieving particular levels of qualifications. Any personal benefit to the learner's own potential was thought secondary to the output of qualifications achieved.

I saw that much provision in the education sector was, and continues to be, actually 'anti-educational'. For many people it provides little more than a lifelong distrust of formal learning experiences with their externally imposed assessments, milestones, targets, outputs, cohorts and so on.

The percentage that 'make-it' educationally to doctorates is very small and how relevant is this to human potential as a whole? By then their level of specialisation within 'the system' is entrenched. It often prevents any innovative thinking and any questioning of that system. Mostly, an 'integrative', holistic approach is needed to innovate and this is unlikely within a specialist and often dogmatic framework of reference. Creative input into the educational system is blocked and has been since the last Educational Reform Act. Even the then Secretary of State for Education, was heard to utter concerns about the future of creativity in learning.

Dr. A Bartlett Giamatti was once President of Yale University and included in a freshman address.

"I believe a liberal education is an education in the root meaning of liberal - liber, 'free - the liberty of the mind free to explore itself, free to draw itself out, to connect with other minds and spirits in the quest for truth. Its goal is to train the whole person to be at once intellectually discerning and humanly flexible, tough-minded and open hearted; to be responsive to the new and responsible for values that make us civilised. It is to teach us to meet what is new and different with reasoned judgement and humanity.

Education in its ideal sense is a positive force for human evolution, in that if we are 'going somewhere', as individuals, communities or as a species, it can help us discover the way. My own experience as a college lecturer is that formal education generally seems to be getting further away from this 'discovery' ideal and more rigid and dogmatic in its application, although there are notable exceptions to this, usually found in unique teachers who are adaptive to the situation and fired-up with their subject.

Having studied teaching at a post-graduate level, and having worked as an adult educator for ten years or so, I became aware of how the education system we have often puts people off wanting to learn anything for their entire lives. Yet learning is a very natural part of being human. We hardly need institutions for this. We learn quite naturally from each other and a good teacher will enhance this learning process that occurs naturally between people.

When I was teaching the 'imposed curriculum' at 'A' level and beyond (16 years plus) I would often think of something called 'gavage'. The college was an exam factory and the students are like the geese who produce 'Pate de Foi Gras', the teachers engaged in an act of 'mental gavage', massaging their minds instead of their throats and cramming their brains with information and techniques to pass the exams so the college can maximise funding.

The root idea of 'education' comes from the root Latin word 'educere' – to 'lead out' to extend the mind – was long gone in an institution that like nearly every other is now fiscally managed and led. I left my employ at that college in order to set up a learning centre based in a community centre where I lived.

Community based learning follows Greek patterns rather than the Roman. For example Socratic dialogue is a formal method by which a small group (5-15 people), guided by a facilitator, find precise answers to a universal question. In the Roman model, a pedagog is someone who educates people. The educator, academic, faculty member, academician, an educator who works at a college or university is the expert responsible for 'passing down' the information to their hopefully eager-eared and receptive students.

Community Governance

"What we now want most is closer contact and better understanding between individuals and communities all over the earth and the elimination of that

fanatical devotion to exalted ideas of national egoism and pride, which is always prone to plunge the world into primeval barbarism and strife."

Nikola Tesla

"Postmodern society thwarts our innate desire to participate politically, just voting in an election every few years, marching once in a while, or signing petitions on Avaaz or MoveOn doesn't count for much. We need new avenues for passionate participation – not just in elections every few years, but continuously. The desire for this is so effectively masked and covered up that most people don't even feel it as something they have forfeited.

Today's communications infrastructure could support a permanent revolution. In fact, I think this would be its logical endpoint. It seems possible – let's try a thought experiment – to design and launch a social networking infrastructure, via the internet, that seamlessly supports political collaboration, direct democracy and resource sharing, based on transparent exchanges. Along with launching a global platform, we would need to undertake a mass educational initiative through the media. We would have to disseminate the values and principles of a cooperative, trust-based society to people across the world."

Daniel Pinchbeck How Soon is Now?

In the UK we already have a locally-based government in the form of our parish and town councils. Positions at these councils are filled by 'representative democracy' also, but at 'bottom end' of the system of government there is much better potential for actual representation at a local level. At this level democracy works well and I say that as someone who has worked as a parish clerk for ten years.

Elections are held every four years and these local bodies come complete with model sets of governance, codes of conduct, financial regulations and strategies to keep them independent and transparent, even an annual audit. Everything you need to activate a community except the political will. They are funded from the Council Tax paid by local residents.

Often the membership is slanted towards the well-off, the retired and unfortunately, some who enjoy the sound of their own voice. They seem to exist quite often without defined or directional leadership,

178

without a 'vision' for their community and they seemingly support political the status quo and innovate very little.

The National Association of Local Councils website states:

"Parish councils are the most local tier of government – they're at the very heart of the community, giving neighbourhoods a voice and helping people feel more involved in the decisions that affect them. They take localism to the next level by giving people a democratic voice that goes beyond just voting in elections. And yet, only a third of the population is covered by one. We want to change this and see more of England join the tens and thousands of parish councils already in existence."

Independents for Frome (IfF) was created to support a group of individuals to stand and get elected to Frome Town Council in 2011. Ten of the seventeen who stood were elected. This gave IfF an outright majority on the council that allowed a raft of ambitious ideas to be implemented much of which is described in '*Flatpack Democracy'* [A DIY guide to creating independent politics by Peter Macfadyen]. Independents for Frome had 27 people wishing to stand in 2011 and selected 17 all of whom were elected – with every seat heavily contested. They are now engaged in an even more ambitious programme for Frome.

One of the keys to their success is that the group operate a 'Way of Working' . This enables them to make decisions in the best interest of Frome, while not emulating the Party Political system that they feel is counter-productive at Parish/Town level. More details of the Way of Working and other aspects of their success can be found in our book '*Flatpack Democracy*'.

Many of the initial party have been engaged with conversations, workshops, meetings and events in Frome for over a decade. Working on themselves and others in the slow unravelling of the stories we've been told about growth, happiness through consumption and the possibility that we can continue to live as we have done for decades. This work has often been linked Joanna Macy's 'work that reconnects' that forces engagement with humankind's insane distruction of our biosphere. And to that of the Transition Town Movement. Transition has focussed minds on climate change, peak oil and the limits to growth all over the world – perhaps in doing so it has helped create foundations from which the dedicated action of Extinction Rebellion will really take hold in the next few weeks… and perhaps that will force a government which continues to demonstrate a complete and utter contempt for their moral duty towards future generations, to turn and face the catastrophe approaching. By operating broadly as normal people do in normal everyday life, they have taken the opportunities presented by Localism whilst looking for ways to change, for the better, the relationships between people and those they elect."

https://www.flatpackdemocracy.co.uk/

British style of politics has been to leave decision making to the politicians and the professions/ bureaucrats with a periodic election thrown in. Indifference has become a deep-rooted part of our political culture, and judging by the recent local elections it is still flourishing. How long can we live with such a busted democratic flush?

We can of course build a more active, knowledgeable and engaged community, where citizens gradually adopt roles as movers and shakers rather than mere recipients of services. We have hardly scratched the surface in Frome with participatory grant making, citizen's panels, skill's networks et al but already intriguing enigmas are emerging. They will be familiar to many of you, a more participatory form of governance throws into immediate relief questions about representation , leadership, legitimacy, authority and archaic regulations. All questions which are as old as the debates about democracy itself but bizarrely more acute at this the lowest of tiers. Just where you would expect most flexibility there are constraints and hidden bear traps. Thanks god for the power of general competence, although even that is not quite the panacea it might have first seemed.

Secondly, can we ditch the idea that our council and all of its trapping and paraphernalia are the equivalent of a vending machine, you drop in your pound coin as taxes or fees and expect the machine to dispense at least £1 in services. When the machine inevitably malfunctions, delivering pop tarts instead of mars bars, the natural tendency like Basil Fawlty is to give the machine a "damn good thrashing".

Ultimately, this model undermines people's confidence in, and their allegiance to local government. In fact the core business of localities should be solving problems, not delivering services. Providing services is only one aspect of an innovative, and at times risky, problem-solving approach that must engage citizens to be effective.

Article from Mel Usher from the National Association of Local Council's (NALC) Magazine

Endpiece

I started this book with a discussion of the purpose of humans. To my mind human beings are a miracle. Billions of little blobs of consciousness on a random planet near a random star in an infinite Universe. The odds of us evolving into what we are and the tiny 'window for life' this planet allows are infinitessimally small.

We have evolved quite quickly and changed the conditions it took to nurture us into being. Many of us are stuck in a paradigm where the environment is our enemy, the earth is here to be dominated and conquered and only the fittest and meanest can survive. But many of us are also in the process of a Spiritual Renaissance, discovering for ourselves a place in the cosmos, a true meaning for our existence.

Unfortunately those who are stuck seem to be making the rules for us all. Governments first formed to protect and help people are now perpetrators of massive conflict. The UK and US governments are run by puppets and controlled by economic interests, the side-effects of which are killing our planet. Our sovereignty and personal freedoms have been sold. We are all in massive financial debt. Through the dishonesty of the financial institutions we are all told that austerity, limit, hardship are the norm. The pirates have taken over and are plundering everything, destroying our air, our water, our food, our privacy, our ability to evolve as spiritual beings in a physical universe.

Democracy has become a lie, a circus to make us think we still have some choice in the matter of being governed. The 'free market' rules and creates massive oppression globally, hurting most the people least able to protect themselves from its ingress.

The system is so ingrained it perpetrates its lies though every institution, enforcing the norms through both legislation and myths of 'normative behaviour', even though our written and spoken language, designed to control and keep people willing servants of the system without question.

But people are waking up. The uneasy feelings of cognitive dissonance are becoming normal as people compare what they think and what they are led to believe, with what they see. Although hundreds of thousands are now awake, it is still not enough to reach the tipping points and make the change a global one. On the one hand, species extinction, environmental breakdown and climate chaos caused by a culture of wetikos mindset, and on the other, people waking from their sleep and finding they are in an entrenched system incapable of change, a leviathan taking us all to the precipice. In the middle, billions of sleepers, deniers, people who feel powerless or people who don't really care.

How can our corrupted democracies be changed? There seems little slack in the system for such change. The archaic, blundering, inefficient and plain crooked governments we have would be more effective with a random lottery of people placed in power. A complete change is needed. The time has come for people to represent themselves through a directly participative democracy. The technology to manage this in an Age of Communication is at hand.

It would seem a time of chaos is unavoidable as the socio-economic system we have has its death-grip on us all, just as nature comes in to bat. We need to resist the control, detach from being governed by refusing to accept their false narratives, contrived for control. We are not just part of culture – we are part of nature too and rediscovering our relationship with it takes us out of their control.

There are many ways to detach and resist but those of us who are awake need to work with each other. There are many opportunities for governing ourselves to starve out the hungry ghosts who have taken over running our world. There are already systems in place for money, exchange, sharing, making food and homes, rediscovering a love of being that brings us closer to finding our real purpose as walking miracles.

All of the answers we need are with us already. Do we endorse a world that protects life or one that destroys life? Do we work for a civilisation that values money and materialism or one that values the complex, interwoven ecosystems that underpin our life and growth on this wondrous planet?

Make your choice now and act accordingly, because your government is elsewhere.

Appendix1: agencies who can access your private data

The full list of agencies that can now ask for UK citizens' internet browsing history, which is laid out in Schedule 4 of the Bill as collected by Chris Yiu:

Metropolitan Police Service

City of London Police

Police forces maintained under section 2 of the Police Act 1996

Police Service of Scotland

Police Service of Northern Ireland

British Transport Police

Ministry of Defence Police

Royal Navy Police

Royal Military Police

Royal Air Force Police

Security Service

Secret Intelligence Service

GCHQ

Ministry of Defence

Department of Health

Home Office

Ministry of Justice

National Crime Agency

HM Revenue & Customs

Department for Transport

Department for Work and Pensions

NHS trusts and foundation trusts in England that provide ambulance services

Common Services Agency for the Scottish Health Service

Competition and Markets Authority

Criminal Cases Review Commission

Department for Communities in Northern Ireland

Department for the Economy in Northern Ireland

Department of Justice in Northern Ireland

Financial Conduct Authority

Fire and rescue authorities under the Fire and Rescue Services Act 2004

Food Standards Agency

Food Standards Scotland

Gambling Commission

Gangmasters and Labour Abuse Authority

Health and Safety Executive

Independent Police Complaints Commissioner

Information Commissioner

NHS Business Services Authority

Northern Ireland Ambulance Service Health and Social Care Trust

Northern Ireland Fire and Rescue Service Board

Northern Ireland Health and Social Care Regional Business Services Organisation

Office of Communications

Office of the Police Ombudsman for Northern Ireland

Police Investigations and Review Commissioner

Scottish Ambulance Service Board

Scottish Criminal Cases Review Commission

Serious Fraud Office

Welsh Ambulance Services National Health Service Trust

Appendix 2: Language meta model

Joseph O'Connor and John Seymour take this deconstruction of language even further in their book *'Introducing Neuro Linguistic Programming, The New Psychology of Personal Excellence'*.

In the practice of intellectual self-defense their Meta Model reconnects language with experience, and can be used for gathering information, clarifying meanings, identifying limitations and opening up choices. This is an extremely powerful model for revealing the underlying 'wetiko' patterns in people's preconceived and unexamined ideologies.

Challenge 1. Deletions, nouns: Unspecified noun eg Who or what specifically...?

Examples: 'They are out to get me.' *'Who is?'*

'It's a matter of opinion.' *'What is?'*

'The neighbourhood has been ruined.' *'Who ruined it, how, when, why?'*

'If you leave chocolate around, people eat it.' *'Which people, why?'*

Challenge 2. Deletions, verbs: Unspecified verb eg Who or what specifically...? How specifically is this happening?

Examples: 'He travelled to Paris.' *'How did he travel?'*

'She hurt herself.' *'How did she hurt herself?'*

'I am trying to remember it.' *'How are you trying to remember it?'*

'What specifically are you trying to remember anyway?'

Challenge 3. Comparison: 'Compared with what?'

Examples: 'New improved Fluffo washing powder is better.' *'Better than what?'*

'I handled that meeting badly.' '*Compared with what?*'

Challenge 4. Judgement: Who says ..?

Examples: 'I am a selfish person'. '*Who says you are a selfish person?*'
'I do.' '*By what standard do you judge yourself to be..?*'

Challenge 4. Nominalisation

How is this being done? Who is nominalising about what, and how are they doing it?

Description: When a verb describing an ongoing process has been turned into a noun.

eg if a noun cannot be touched, tasted, smelt, seen or heard, it is a nominalisation.

Example: **Teaching** and **discipline**, applied with **respect** and **firmness** are essentials in the **process** of education.

Challenge 5. Generalisations

1. *Modal operator of possibility*: What prevents you..?

Description: Words which set limits governed by unspoken rules,

Example: 'cannot' 'must not'. They define what is considered possible.

2. *Modal operator of necessity*: What would happen if you did/didn't'..?

Description: Involving a need, there is a rule of conduct operating but not explicit.

Example: 'I must always put other people first.' '*What would happen if you didn't?*'

'You shouldn't talk to those people.' '*What would happen if you did?*'

3. *Universal quantifier* Always? Never? Everyone?

Description: Taking a few instances as representing the whole group.

Example: Pop music is rubbish. All generalisations are wrong. Actors are interesting people.

Challenge 6. Distortions

1. *Complex equivalence.* How does this mean that?

Description: Statements linked in such a way they are taken to mean the same thing.

People may generalise their own experience to include everyone and forget that others think in different ways.

Example: 'You are not smiling...you are not enjoying yourself.'

'If you don't look at me when I'm talking to you, then you are not paying attention.'

2. *Presupposition.* What leads you to believe that..?

Description: Basic assumptions which limit choice.

Example: 'Are you going to wear your green pyjamas or the red ones to go to bed?

'What leads you to believe I am going to bed?'

'When you get smart, you'll understand this.'

'Why don't you smile more?'

3. *Cause and effect:* How exactly does that make this happen?

Description: Assumptions that one thing causes another, eg 'You made me do it'(Eric Berne)

Examples: 'You made me feel angry.' 'The weather gets me down.' ' You bore me.'

4. *Mind Reading:* How do you know..?

Description: Presuming to know how another feels.

Example: 'I could tell she didn't like the present I gave her.'

'He was angry but he wouldn't admit it.'

Also mirrors: 'If you cared for me you would know what I wanted.'

'Can't you see how I feel?'

'You should know that I like that.'

"Which meta-model violation you challenge will depend on the context of the communication and your outcome. Consider the following sentence.

' Why don't these awful people stop always trying to help me, it makes me even angrier; I

know I should keep my temper, but I can't.'

This contains mind reading and presupposition (they are trying to annoy me), cause and effect (makes), universal quantifiers (always), judgements (awful), comparisons (angrier), modal operators of possibility and necessity (should, can't), unspecified verbs (trying and help), nominalisation (temper), and unspecified nouns (people, it).

Source books

Boyle M. Drinking Molotov Cocktails With Ghandi. Permanent Publications. 2015

Boyle M. The Moneyless Manifesto, Live Well, Live Rich, Live Free. Permanent Publications. 2012

Brand R. Revolution. Century

Corby R. Re-Wild Yourself, Becoming Nature. Amanita Forrest. 2015

Dauncey G. Journey to the Future. Ingram Books. 2016

Edwards D. Free to be Human, Intellectual Self-Defense in an Age of Illusions. Green Books. 1995

Edwards D. The Compassionate Revolution, Radical Politics and Buddhism. Green Books. 1998

Eliot J. Action Research for Educational Change. OU Press 1992

Griffiths J. Wild: An Elemental Journey. Hamish Hamilton. 2006

Icke D. The Robots' Rebellion, The Story of the Spiritual Renaissance. Gateway Books. 1994

Klein N. This Changes Everything, Capitalism vs. The Climate. Penguin. 2014

Knowles M. The Adult Learner, A Neglected Species. Gulf. 1990.

Levy P. Dispelling Wetiko, Breaking the Curse of Evil. North Atlantic Books. 2013

Lovelock J.E. Gaia, A New Look at Life on Earth. Oxford University Press. 1979

Lucas C. Honourable Friends? Parliament and the Fight For Change. Portobello.

Macy J. & Johnstone C. Active Hope, How to Face the Mess We Are In Without Going Crazy. New World Library. 2012.

Russell P. The Awakening Earth, The Global Brain. Arkana. 1982